GOLDEN YEARS OF
BASEBALL

JOE
DIMAGGIO
Outfield

YANKEES

ERNIE
BANKS
CHICAGO CUBS   SS

OUTFIELD
TWINS

TONY
OLIVA

MICKEY
MANTLE
N. Y. YANKEES   OF

GOLDEN YEARS OF
BASEBALL

JIM KAPLAN
FOREWORD BY RED BARBER

Crescent Books
New York/Avenel, New Jersey

This 1992 edition published by Crescent Books, distributed by Outlet Book Company, Inc., a Random House Company, 40 Engelhard Avenue Avenel, New Jersey 07001

Produced by Brompton Books Corporation 15 Sherwood Place Greenwich, CT 06830

ISBN 0-517-06983-0

8 7 6 5 4 3 2

Printed and bound in Hong Kong

Page 1: *The 1924 world champion Washington Senators pose in Griffith Stadium. Dwarfing "boy" manager Bucky Harris on his left, pitcher Walter "Big Train" Johnson is front and center.*

Page 2: *An All-Star array of bubblegum delights from the '40s, '50s and '60s.* **Top from left:** *Nellie Fox, Joe DiMaggio, Ernie Banks.* **Middle:** *Tony Oliva, Al Rosen, Duke Snider.* **Bottom:** *Ralph Kiner, Monte Irvin, Mickey Mantle.*

Below: *Joe Gordon singles home DiMaggio and Lou Gehrig while the Yankees beat the Cubs 5-2 to win their third straight game in the 1938 World Series.*

CONTENTS

FOREWORD

Golden Years of Baseball is not only a wonderfully interesting baseball book, it is also an historic perspective. The game you see today is not the way baseball was played and ordered years ago. Jim Kaplan has written clearly, and the wealth of pictures assembled gives this book a watershed view. I began broadcasting in 1930 and am still on network radio. I broadcast in 1934 from an airplane when the Reds flew to Chicago (the first time a major league team traveled by air), did the first night game in 1935, the first TV game in 1939, was at Brooklyn when Jackie Robinson came, relayed Lavagetto's hit and Gionfriddo's catch in 1947, Bobby Thomson's home run and Maris's 61st. I know what this book is all about.

The golden decades begin in 1919, just when it seemed baseball might well be finished as a national sport. Eight Chicago White Sox players were involved in throwing certain World Series games so that gamblers might profit. When this news broke in 1920 the nation was stunned and sickened. Until then baseball had just run along without strong direction. It was still a loosely organized sport for the good old boys. But now, no longer.

Frightened club owners knew they had to get one man of impeccable honesty and strength, and turn the game over to him. They wisely chose Federal Judge Kenesaw Mountain Landis. Landis immediately barred for life the eight players. Landis took over as a czar, and not only ran the game but gave it back its integrity.

At the same time one ballplayer gave baseball an excitement it had never known. Babe Ruth hit 59 home runs in 1920, and he hit them high and far, and in all ball parks. So it was, out of the darkness of 1919 came a brightness baseball had not expected or experienced. The golden decades began.

Today we see games in huge stadiums, played by players who are paid fortunes, and played before the television camera. This book brings you back to when the major leagues were 16 teams – all but one east of the Mississippi – when travel was by train, radio was barred in New York, TV never thought about, and certainly only white men would play.

Golden Years of Baseball covers not only the star players of the 50-year period from 1919 to 1969, it also brings forth the changes in our country that brought changes to the game: airplanes – especially the jet, which made expansion even to the Pacific coast possible – radio and television, the population explosion, the automobile, and World War II.

In my opinion five men dominated 1919-1969. I was fortunate to know them and to know their lasting impact on baseball. I have mentioned two, Landis and Ruth. The other three are Branch Rickey, Larry MacPhail and Marvin Miller.

From the time of Judge Landis the first duty of the commissioner of baseball has been to keep gambling out of baseball. This was the bottom line of the Pete Rose tragedy.

Babe Ruth did more than hit home runs and provide a fresh excitement. Ruth changed the way the game was played, and is still being played today. The home run, the big hit, became the game. Ruth changed batting philosophy as well as technique; swing a lighter bat and from the end. Ruth not only built Yankee Stadium, he created a new style of baseball.

This book has marvelous pictures of Ted Williams, Ty Cobb, Rogers Hornsby, Walter Johnson, Carl Hubbell, John McGraw, Connie Mack, George Sisler, Roger Maris, Leo Durocher, Joe DiMaggio, Willie Mays, Roy Campanella, Larry Doby, Henry Aaron, Bob Gibson and many others, but none of these men changed baseball. They brightened it, yes indeed, but left no lasting impact. Jackie Robinson, by his physical and spiritual abilities, showed how a black man could play in the major leagues, and be a tremendous gate attraction, but the change – the decision to break the color line – came from Branch Rickey. However, if I were to name a sixth man who changed baseball, it would be Jackie Robinson.

Rickey turned poverty into plenty. He had such a down-and-out team at St. Louis that he had to figure out how to have good teams without money. He couldn't buy players as the rich teams could and did. He created the farm system. He sent his scouts across the country to search for young, untried boys. He placed them on various minor league teams with managers who were teachers. He waited with patience until these boys became men, until they matured. When they did, his Cardinals in 1926 defeated the mighty Yankees built with Jake Ruppert's money. Soon all the other teams had to have their own farm systems. The other mighty and enduring change by Rickey was to single-handedly bring black players into the minor leagues. Black players are now extremely prominent in many starting teams, have become stars and made possible the expansion from 16 to 26 teams, with two more to come.

Larry MacPhail was a shooting star. He was in the majors 11 years – three at Cincinnati, five at Brooklyn and three at Yankee Stadium. He rebuilt all three franchises. He pioneered air travel, radio, television, night ball and the season ticket plan, plus broadcasting live all his games in New York.

Until Marvin Miller came along in 1966 to weld a baseball players' union, the players were under the reserve clause – they were owned for life and had to take or leave what the owners would pay them – or get out of baseball. Take it or leave it. Many times the players had tried to form an association by themselves and got nowhere. Miller in 1966 first sold the players on a union, then used the strength of the union to break the reserve clause, to have arbitration, free agency, and skilled agents to negotiate. Television and bigger stadiums came along with the money, and Miller's union saw to it the players got their share.

Yes, this is a wonderful book. It brings together the changing, maturing 50 years – from 1919 to 1969 – that created baseball today. But as you see this book, and see a game, be sure to still see Judge Landis, Babe Ruth, Branch Rickey (and Jackie Robinson), Larry MacPhail and Marvin Miller.

RED BARBER

INTRODUCTION

What makes the 50-year period between 1919 and 1969 baseball's Golden Decades? Certainly there's room for debate. Some might prefer the first two decades of the century, when Ty Cobb was stealing bases aplenty, Walter Johnson and Christy Mathewson were plowing 'em down aplenty, and runs were earned by "scientific baseball" instead of free swinging. More modern fans could tout the 1970s, when Pete Rose was the prime hustling player and Reggie Jackson the prime October player. Nineteenth-century buffs could preach the virtues of the really old days, when baseball seemed to be growing and changing every day.

But 1919-69 still wins the brass ring. For one thing, money wasn't really a factor in baseball then. Granted, players were underpaid and prone to complain and hold out and such, but by and large we could still concentrate on the game between the lines. Cash and commercialism hadn't obscured our vision yet.

Two of our chosen decades have already been called the Golden Age of Baseball. They were the 1920s, when the Babe and Mr. McGraw were in their heyday and balls started flying out of the yard in droves, and the 1950s, when Willie, Mickey and the Duke gave us nonstop thrills.

The other three decades we've chosen weren't exactly slackers either. In the 1930s baseball went full steam ahead while the rest of society sometimes seemed to be going nowhere; to many, baseball was the tonic for what ailed them. The 1940s, which have become very fashion-able of late, gave us baseball's best season (1941) and best news (integration), too. The 1960s seemed to boast one miracle after another, from the miraculous Maz to the Miracle Red Sox and Miracle Mets.

The 1919-69 period is of particular interest to scholars, because it encompassed years of profound change. If you don't believe us, just consider the differences between 1919 and 1969.

Imagine baseball in 1919. The game is played exclusively in the northeast quadrant of the country, and teams travel by train. Dressed in baggy flannel uniforms, the players are virtually all white Americans, with an occasional Native American or light-skinned Hispanic on the diamond. The ball isn't very white at all. Tobacco juice, licorice, spit, sweat, bat marks – all have left their signature on a ball that may be in use the entire game. As might be expected, it's a pitcher's dream. He throws legal wet ones that take crazy routes to the strike zone. Even when it's hit, the ball doesn't carry very far. While outfielders breathe down infielders' necks, the hitting team must scheme for runs any way possible – with suicide squeezes and stolen bases and sacrifices and savvy. The game is watched almost exclusively by men in white shirts, suits and hats. They must be a knowledgeable crowd, because there are no public-address loudspeakers or numbers or names on uniforms to identify the players. Fortunately, the paying customers are seated close to the players in intimate urban parks. Ballpark fans are the only ones to follow the game as it

Page 6: *Hall-of-Fame broadcaster Red Barber witnessed everything from the first night game to the first integrated game in baseball history.*

Opposite: *The Yanks' Billy Martin is forced out at second as Dodger shortstop Pee Wee Reese takes the throw in Game Six of the 1955 World Series. The Yankees won 5-1.*

Right: *Pittsburgh's Bill Mazeroski is mobbed by jubilant teammates and fans after his ninth-inning home run in Game Seven won the 1960 Pirates-Yankees World Series.*

Oct 2, 1932

CHICAGO ⑥ NEW YORK ⑬
(4TH GAME)

WORLD'S SERIES

1 9 3 2

CHICAGO CUBS
vs.
NEW YORK YANKEES

CHICAGO
NATIONAL
LEAGUE
BALL CLUB

WRIGLEY FIELD

Souvenir
SCORE CARD
25¢

Left: *The action was as colorful as the programs in the 1932 World Series, especially when New York's Babe Ruth hit his celebrated "called shot" homer off Cub pitcher Charlie Root.*

Opposite top left: *Acquired by the Cubs from the Reds in 1949, Hank Sauer went on to have his best season in Chicago in 1952, when he led the National League in homers and RBIs, winning the MVP Award.*

Opposite top right: *Hall of Famer Warren Spahn hurled his magic for the Braves – in both Boston and Milwaukee – for 20 years, winning 20 or more games 13 times.*

Opposite bottom: *During the 1955 season Brooklyn sluggers (from left) Duke Snider, Gil Hodges, Roy Campanella and Carl Furillo clubbed 127 homers. By October the Dodgers were Bums no more.*

happens, because there is no radio coverage and television hasn't been invented. The public hears what happened through word of mouth and newspapers.

It is 1969. The game is coast-to-coast and Canadian. Teams fly from one city to another. Wearing orlon-and-wool uniforms, the players are from many ethnic backgrounds. With spitters and shiners banned and new balls constantly put in play, the sphere is a gleaming white. There are plenty of similarities to 1919-style play – stolen bases have returned from a long vacation and scientific managing never departed – but Dr. Longball is increasingly seen as the panacea for all batting ills. Gaily dressed men and women dot the stands. You sure can tell the players without a scorecard, because the P.A. announcer introduces each one and they have names or numbers on

their backs. That's a good thing, because fans are farther from the players in the new ballparks, some of which are in the suburbs. You don't have to be at the park to enjoy the fun, since radio and television coverage abound.

In between 1919 and 1969 was a turbulent, uneven period, but one in which baseball rode out the worst crises. In 1919 eight members of the White Sox allegedly conspired to throw the World Series. Even as the news of their indictments broke the next year and naysayers were forecasting the game's doom, Babe Ruth and the home run were about to send baseball to new peaks of prosperity and popularity. In 1968 batting averages were sinking like a ship in a cyclone. A couple of adjustments between seasons, and baseball was as good as gold.

Good as the Golden Decades.

Is there any sport that regenerates itself faster than baseball? Consider the 1920 season, when our national pastime was at its lowest ebb. By late summer two devastating events had shaken public confidence. Carl Mays, the submarining Yankee righthander, killed Cleveland's Ray Chapman with a pitch on August 16; no player before or since has been felled in the line of duty. Of equal consequence, the news was breaking on front pages everywhere that eight members of the Chicago White Sox had conspired to throw the 1919 World Series to underdog Cincinnati. Although they were subsequently cleared in court, all eight would be banned from baseball for life by the sport's first commissioner, Kenesaw Mountain Landis. To use a boxing metaphor, baseball was on the ropes and in danger of being knocked out of the national sporting ring.

And yet the staggering game righted itself. Landis's role in rescuing baseball will forever be debated; the commissioner was as high-handed and arrogant as he was forceful. What is beyond debate is the game's role in rescuing itself. It's plain fact that the 1920 season was as wonderful as it was disquieting. On May 1 Brooklyn's Leon Cadore and the Braves' Joe Oeschger hooked up in baseball's longest game – a 26-inning 1-1 tie. That was an aberration, because the big news was offense. Suddenly, the game was transformed into a spectacle of homers and high-average hitting. At the center of the storm – no surprise – was Babe Ruth. Late of the Red Sox, the new Yankee outfielder upped his major-league homer record from 29 to 54 while his team set a home attendance record of 1,298,422. National League batters hit .274 and American Leaguers .283, while homers were up 46 percent over 1917. The pennant races were splendiferous, and the World Series – featuring Bill Wambsganss's unassisted triple play in the Cleveland victory over Brooklyn – was a gem.

The 1920 season was less a fluke than a forecast. The next year Ruth had his best all-around season (.378 average, 59 homers, 171 runs batted in) and the Yankees and Giants played the first of three consecutive ballyhooed World Series, the last punctuated by Casey Stengel's comic-opera lurch around the bases on an inside-the-park home run. Indeed, every year had some gem of a postseason. In 1924 popular Washington pitcher Walter Johnson finally got his world championship; almost everyone reveled in it, even some members of the losing Giants. "The good Lord couldn't bear to see a fine fellow like Walter Johnson lose again," said Giant pitcher Jack Bentley. In 1925 the Pirates rallied from a three-games-to-one deficit – another baseball first – to beat the Senators. The following season Grover Cleveland Alexander struck out Tony Lazzeri with the bases loaded in the finale to help the Cardinals upset the Yanks. Dusting off the defeat like lint off their shoulders, the 1927 Yankees – perhaps the greatest team of all time – shut out the Pirates. In 1928 the Yanks got revenge and then some over the Cardinals by kayoing them in four straight. The decade ended when Athletic manager Connie Mack, the Tall Tactician, masterminded a Series win over the Cubs by trotting out surprise Game One starter Howard Ehmke, who struck out 13 to set a new Series record. In Game Five, three A's runs in the bottom of the ninth brought a dramatic end to the Series.

According to longstanding legend, the "lively" baseball and the Bambino ushered in the longball era. In *Big Sticks*, William Curran whacks that theory out of the park. There was no known adjustment to the ball between the introduction of the cork center in 1910 and the cushioned-cork center in 1926, he reports. Why so many homers? Three big reasons: 1) In the 1919-20 offseason the Rules Committee outlawed the use of foreign substances on baseballs (except by 17 spitball pitchers who

Pages 12-13: *The Philadelphia Athletics' Max Bishop crosses the plate ahead of Mule Haas, who had just homered to tie the fifth game of the 1929 Series at 2-2. Soon afterwards Bing Miller doubled home Al Simmons with the Series-winning run, to defeat the Cubs four games to one.*

Left: *The Senators' Walter Johnson at bat during the 1925 World Series. The 38-year-old went 1-for-11 at the plate, and pitched three complete Series games, winning two of them but losing the clincher to Pittsburgh.*

Opposite: *A's teammates rush onto the field to congratulate Miller after his Series-ending double in 1929.*

were given a grandfather clause); 2) the next year they ruled that only clean balls could be kept in play; and, 3) the swing-for-the-fences batting style popularized by Ruth put more balls – and fans – in the seats.

Purists blanched. Gone, they squealed, was the "scientific" school of choking up on the bat, poking balls through holes, stealing bases and generally earning runs. Nonsense, argues Curran: ". . .the scientific game had not disappeared at all. There were simply fewer low-scoring games. It's true that in the 1920s base stealing declined rapidly as an offensive weapon. At the same time, the principal features of inside baseball – the sacrifice bunt, the squeeze play, the hit-and-run – along with a variety of defensive strategies – had never lost favor and are still in use today."

If hitters were unscientifically swinging away, why did batting averages soar and strikeout totals decline in the twenties? No one has an adequate explanation for that – not even Curran, although he suggests that bigger and stronger hitters were blasting shellshocked pitchers every which way. Rogers Hornsby, who set the century's single-season mark with a .424 average in 1924, said that only the best hitters were swinging away. Presumably, the rest were benefiting from cleaner balls and disciplined hitting styles.

But the decade shouldn't be derided for poor pitching. The very assault on moundsmen resulted in the first widespread usage of perhaps the most devastating gun in the pitching arsenal – the relief pitcher. Nor should we overlook fielding. When Spittin' Bill Doak sold the Raw-

lings Company on a new glove with a preformed pocket, fielders reached new heights. In 1924 Pittsburgh's Glenn Wright, to name just one of the period's outstanding glovemen, set a shortstop record for the 154-game season with 601 assists. And baseball could only improve, now that teams had farm systems.

More people saw baseball games than ever before, and attendance records were set for four consecutive years starting in 1924. People also read and heard more colorful accounts. Harold Arlin announced the first game on radio when Pittsburgh beat Philadelphia 8-5 at Forbes Field on August 5, 1921. If you doubt it was a Golden Age of Sportswriting, witness this sarcastic aside by Paul Gallico: "The jackrabbit ball is with us again. For the benefit of the uninformed, the jackrabbit ball is a baseball that the other side is slugging something scandalous."

All in all, twenties baseball was a delight to anyone but the most nostalgic crank. The game dominated the decade on a par with bathtub gin, flappers and jazz, while the Babe was a national figure every bit the equal of Charles Lindbergh, Al Capone and Jack Dempsey. "People in every big city in the land," Robert Smith wrote in *Baseball*, "suddenly discovered that baseball could be as exciting, in its summery way, as all-night drinking and dancing, airplanes, fast automobiles, and reckless gambling on the Stock Exchange. The Babe became almost a symbol of the age, and his fame was for a time surely unmatched by any figure in sports or out."

Neither baseball nor Ruth crashed with the stock market: they soared. Talk about regeneration!

SCANDAL AND TRAGEDY

Right: *White Sox outfielder Shoeless Joe Jackson was a .356 career hitter who batted .382 in 1920, his last season; his career ended abruptly when he was implicated in the Black Sox scandal.*

Below: *A scene from the 1919 World Series. Cincinnati beat the favored White Sox – some of whom were dogging it – five games to three.*

Opposite top left: *Appointed baseball's first commissioner in 1920, Kenesaw Mountain Landis banned eight members of the White Sox for allegedly conspiring with gamblers to throw the 1919 World Series.*

Opposite top right: *Cleveland shortstop Ray Chapman was killed when a pitch thrown by New York's Carl Mays beaned him in 1920. Though Mays swore he was just trying to throw inside, the pitch may have cost him a spot in the Hall of Fame.*

Opposite bottom: *The 1919 White Sox, a team that shall live in infamy.*

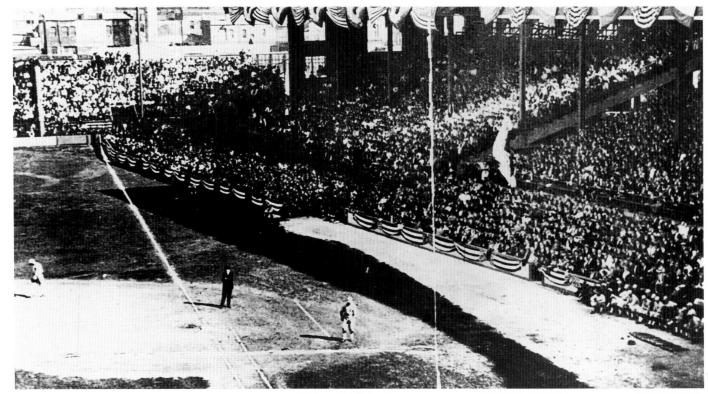

BASEBALL SURVIVES – AND THEN SOME
The 1920 Season

Opposite top: *No wonder Cleveland centerfielder-manager Tris Speaker looks tickled pink before the second game of the 1920 World Series. He's flanked by two Hall of Famers, the incomparable second baseman Napoleon Lajoie (left) and pitcher Cy Young, who was so effective they named an award after him.*

Opposite bottom: *Indian pitcher Jim Bagby is shown losing the second game of the '20 Series. However, he won the classic fifth game and hit the first postseason home run by a pitcher for good measure.*

Right: *Joe Sewell replaced the fallen Chapman as Indian shortstop in 1920. He batted .329 over 22 games, then slumped to .174, with a Series-leading six errors, against Brooklyn.*

Below: *Besides the acquisition of Babe Ruth by the Yankees, the fatal beaning of Ray Chapman, and the 26-inning 1-1 tie pitched by the Dodgers' Leon Cadore and the Braves' Joe Oeschger (baseball's longest game), the other historic event of the 1920 season was the only unassisted triple play in World Series history. Bill Wambsganss (left, with teammate Elmer Smith) turned the trick in Game Four.*

THE LAST OF THE SPITBALL PITCHERS

Opposite: *Burleigh Grimes, one of the last legal spitballers. The longtime Dodger great, who was allowed to continue throwing wet ones after doctored pitches were banned for most players in 1920, won 270 games and was elected to Cooperstown in 1964. He is shown here in a Cubs uniform; he played for them briefly late in his career.*

Right: *The Indians' Stan Coveleski won three games in the 1920 World Series, including the clinching seventh. He allowed only two runs in 27 innings and led all pitchers in that serve-'em-up Series with eight strikeouts. Coveleski was one of 17 spitball pitchers exempted from the spitball ban; the others were Bill Doak, Phil Douglas, Dana Fillingim, Ray Fisher, Marvin Goodwin, Burleigh Grimes, Clarence Mitchell, Duke Rudolph, Doc Ayers, Ray Caldwell, Red Faber, Dutch Leonard, Jack Quinn, Allan Russell, Urban Shocker and Allan Sothoron.*

THE FIRST OF THE SLUGGERS
Power Hitters in the Early Twenties

Opposite: *Hack Wilson, who began his Hall of Fame career with the Giants in 1923, blossomed as a hitter when he joined the Cubs in 1926 and led the league in home runs with 21. Wilson belted a National League record 56 homers and drove in an all-time record 190 runs in 1930.*

Right: *Babe Ruth began the decade with consecutive all-time slugging average records – .847 and .846. Shown here hitting one out in St. Petersburg during 1927 spring training, he went on to homer 60 times during the regular season for a record that stood for 34 years.*

Below: *The slashing Tris Speaker, a .344 hitter for the Red Sox, Indians, Senators and Athletics, had more doubles (223) than strikeouts (220).*

Below right: *Dodger great Zack Wheat, a .317 hitter and leftfielder supreme, made a pre-1961 all-star team chosen by Hall-of-Fame manager Casey Stengel.*

A HITTER'S AGE
High Average Hitters of the Decade

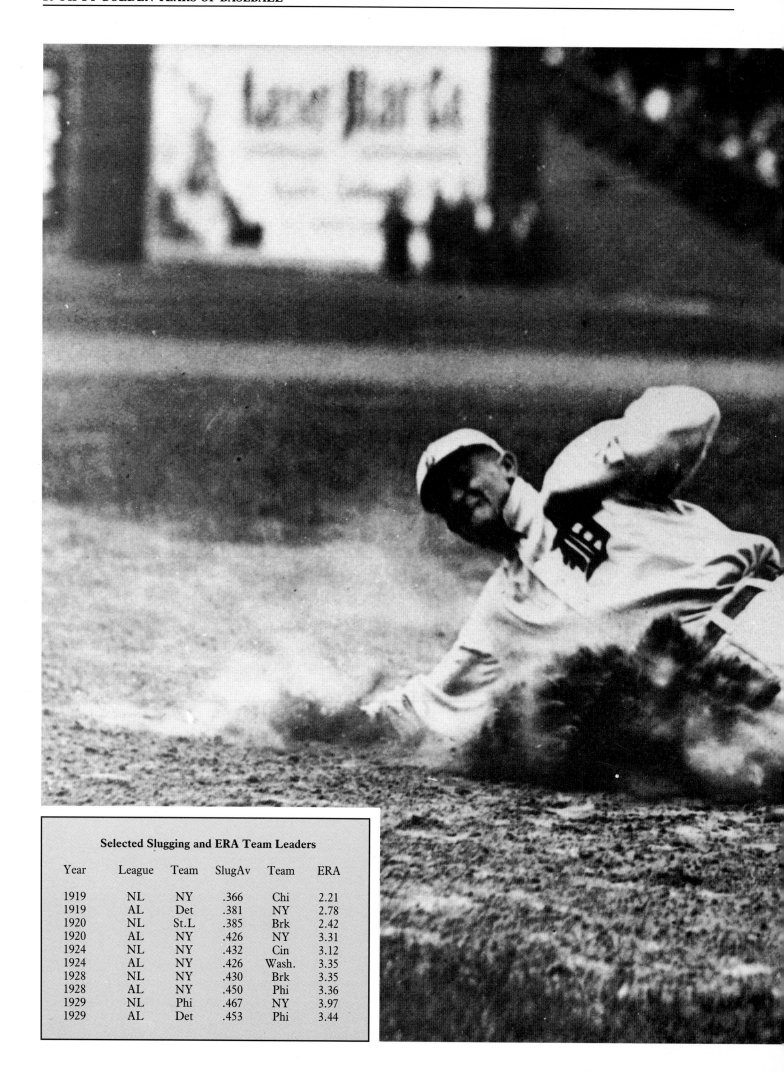

Selected Slugging and ERA Team Leaders

Year	League	Team	SlugAv	Team	ERA
1919	NL	NY	.366	Chi	2.21
1919	AL	Det	.381	NY	2.78
1920	NL	St.L	.385	Brk	2.42
1920	AL	NY	.426	NY	3.31
1924	NL	NY	.432	Cin	3.12
1924	AL	NY	.426	Wash.	3.35
1928	NL	NY	.430	Brk	3.35
1928	AL	NY	.450	Phi	3.36
1929	NL	Phi	.467	NY	3.97
1929	AL	Det	.453	Phi	3.44

BASEBALL ROARS WITH THE TWENTIES

*Showman supreme, Babe Ruth (**opposite,** shown here with his fiance in 1929) was a Roaring Twenties icon on a par with Charles Lindbergh and Al Capone. The only other sporting legends to compete with the Bambino's celebrity were golfer Bobby Jones (**top,** being photographed upon his return as the British Open winner in 1927), the New York Giants' manager John McGraw (**above**) and boxer Jack Dempsey (**right,** sailing on his honeymoon in 1925).*

THE BABE DOES IT ALL

Opposite top: *Babe Ruth presents certificates to Yankee pitcher Waite Hoyt (left) and first baseman Lou Gehrig at the 1928 World Series. This was the year that Christy Walsh, Ruth's advisor, started the Babe Ruth All-American team – an all-star team of the entire major leagues.*

Opposite bottom: *A young Babe Ruth takes batting practice.*

Above: *Always a favorite with children, Ruth is mobbed by young autograph-seekers during an orphanage visit in 1927, the year he hit a then-record 60 homers.*

Right: *The Sultan of Swat takes an uncharacteristic righthanded stance, plainly bested by a nattily outfitted kid clouter.*

Opposite: *Ruth scoring in the 1923 Series. Behind the great man, who batted .368 and led both teams with eight walks, eight runs, three homers and a 1.000 slugging percentage, the Yankees beat the Giants four games to two and won their first world championship.*

Right: *Ruth was the greatest drawing card in baseball history. It even says so on his Hall of Fame plaque. In 1920, when Ruth hit 54 homers, Yankee attendance doubled from the previous year, setting a then-league record of 1,298,422.*

Below: *Ruth, the Mighty Mite – Yankee manager Miller Huggins – and Gehrig plan the 1929 season in St. Petersburg. Alas, after three straight years in first they would have to play second fiddle to Connie Mack's Philadelphia Athletics.*

Copyright by the Press Publishing Company (New York World), 1927

THE GREAT TURNSTILE WHIRLER

—Cassel in the New York *World*.

OH, WHAT A RIVALRY!
Yankees-Giants in the Early Twenties

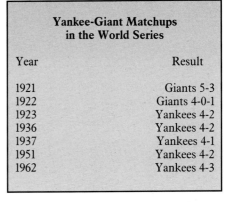

Yankee-Giant Matchups in the World Series	
Year	Result
1921	Giants 5-3
1922	Giants 4-0-1
1923	Yankees 4-2
1936	Yankees 4-2
1937	Yankees 4-1
1951	Yankees 4-2
1962	Yankees 4-3

Opposite: *The inaugural at Yankee Stadium on April 19, 1923. No wonder they called it The House that Ruth Built: Before 70,000 appreciative fans, the Babe hit one out.*

Left top: *The Giants' Frank Snyder and Jesse Barnes score on Dave Bancroft's two-run single in the sixth game of the 1921 Series. The Giants won 8-5, and went on to take the Series from the Yanks, five games to three.*

Left middle: *The Yankees' 1921 American League champions. Ruth (arm around catcher Wally Schang, second row) had his best overall year, hitting .378 and leading the league with 59 homers, 177 runs and 171 runs batted in.*

Left bottom: *Casey Stengel scores on his famous inside-the-park home run to give the Giants a 5-4 victory over the Yankees in the opening game of the 1923 Series.*

MUGGSY'S MEN
Great Giants Who Played Under McGraw

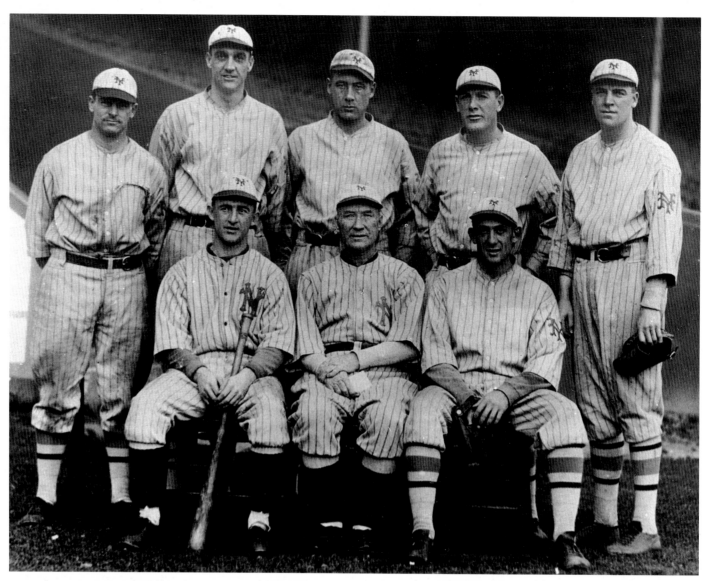

Opposite top: *Members of the 1924 New York Giants taking part in their fourth consecutive World Series. Seated, from left: Frankie Frisch, Coach Hughie Jennings, Art Nehf. Standing: Ross Youngs, George "Highpockets" Kelly, Frank Snyder, Emil "Irish" Meusel, Rosy Ryan.*

Opposite bottom: *Giant third baseman Heinie Groh tags out Cleveland's Tris Speaker in spring training. Groh was known for his odd-shaped "bottle" bat.*

Right: *Travis "Stonewall" Jackson, the Giants' crack shortstop. Jackson took over when Dave Bancroft was traded to the Braves in 1924; Stonewall batted .291 over 15 seasons.*

Below: *Dave Bancroft batting in the 1923 Series. He fielded (1.000) much better than he hit (.083).*

HOW YOU GONNA KEEP 'EM ON THE FARM?
The Cardinals' First Successful Farm System

Cardinal Farm Hands

Player	Position	Career Began	Ended	Cardinals Years	Pennants
*Jim Bottomley	1B	1922	1937	11	4
Tommy Thevenow	SS	1924	1938	5	2
Chick Hafey	OF	1924	1937	8	4
Taylor Douthit	OF	1923	1933	8	3
Bill Hallahan	P	1925	1938	9	4
Charley Gelbert	SS	1929	1940	6	2
Pepper Martin	OF, 3B	1928	1944	13	4
Bill DeLancey	C	1932	1940	4	1
Rip Collins	1B	1931	1941	6	2
*Dizzy Dean	P	1930	1947	7	2
Paul Dean	P	1934	1943	6	1
Tex Carleton	P	1932	1940	3	1
*Joe Medwick	OF	1932	1948	10	1
Terry Moore	OF	1935	1948	11	2
*Johnny Mize	1B	1936	1953	6	0
Mickey Owen	C	1937	1954	4	0
Mort Cooper	P	1938	1949	7	3
Walker Cooper	C	1940	1957	8	3
*Enos Slaughter	OF	1938	1959	13	2
*Stan Musial	OF	1941	1963	22	4
Whitey Kurowski	3B	1941	1949	9	4
Jimmy Brown	INF	1937	1946	7	2
Marty Marion	SS	1940	1953	11	4
Max Lanier	P	1938	1953	12	4
Howard Pollet	P	1941	1956	8	3
Ernie White	P	1940	1948	4	2
Harry Walker	OF	1940	1955	8	3
Alpha Brazle	P	1943	1954	10	2

*Hall of Fame member

Opposite top: *Rogers Hornsby taking batting practice. As playing manager, he led the Cardinals to their first Series title, in 1926.*

Opposite bottom: *Better known as a baseball executive than a .239-hitting catcher, Branch Rickey fathered the modern farm system. The Mahatma's farm system bore fruit beginning in 1926; in the following two decades St. Louis won nine pennants and six World Series.*

Right: *Hornsby managed 14 years.*

Below left: *An early Cardinal farm-system find, first baseman Jim Bottomley had a stellar batting day on September 16, 1924, when he drove in 12 runs with two homers, a double and three singles in a single game.*

Below right: *Outfielder Billy Southworth batted .345 in the 1926 World Series; manager Southworth led the Cardinals to three more pennants in the 1940s.*

QUICK RELIEF

Opposite: *Waite Hoyt was called "Schoolboy" because he signed his first major-league contract at age 15. Mostly, he taught pitching lessons. Over a two-decade career he was 237-182, with a classy 3.59 ERA in a hitter's era. In 1928, his most notable year, he won 23 games and led the American League with eight saves. After his retirement in 1932, Hoyt served as a radio broadcaster and member of the Hall of Fame's Veterans Committee.*

Right: *Manager Bill McKechnie (left) and pitcher Grover Cleveland Alexander in 1928, when the Cardinals won their second pennant. Though Alexander was primarily a starter who won 373 games, his most famous outing was the relief stint that ended the 1926 World Series.*

Below: *Wilcy Moore led the American League twice in saves – with 13 as a Yankee in 1927 and 10 as a Red Sox in 1930.*

Below right: *Clark Griffith won 237 games as a turn-of-the-century pitcher, and developed baseball's first ace relievers, Allan Russell and Firpo Marberry, as the Washington Senators' owner in the 1920s.*

RADIO DAYS
Early Baseball Broadcasting

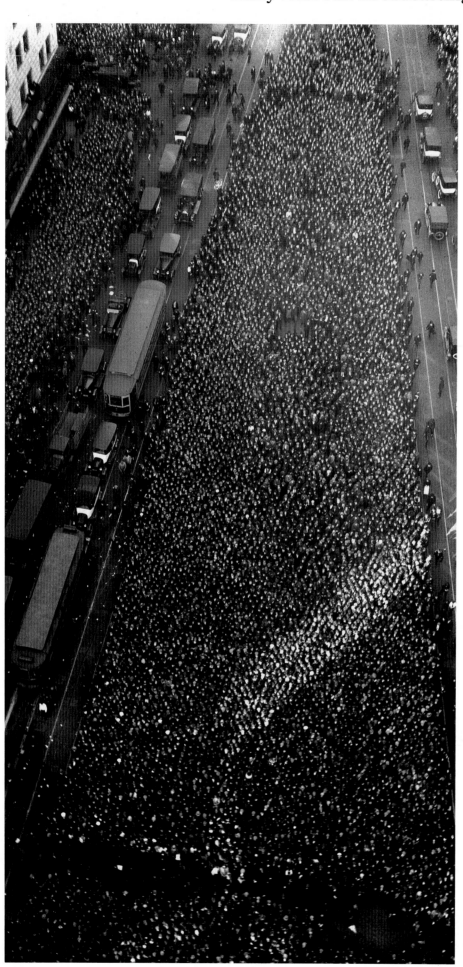

Left: *Crowds watched the scoreboard in New York's Times Square for results of the 1921 World Series.*

Opposite top: *By 1922 three million American homes had a radio. Announcer Graham McNamee, who became a legend with his colorful description of the 1923 World Series, chats with Babe Ruth before the '27 season opener. No less an authority than Red Barber called McNamee "the greatest announcer we ever had."*

Opposite bottom: *Louis Kaufman (center) of radio station KDKA poses in Pittsburgh with some of the 1925 World Champion Pirates (from left): Manager Bill McKechnie, pitcher Lee Meadows, third baseman Pie Traynor, and rightfielder Kiki Cuyler. Four years earlier the first radio broadcast of baseball was heard over KDKA, with Harold Arlin announcing.*

A SERIES OF WONDERS
The 1924 World Series

Opposite top: *The Senators beat the Giants 2-1 in Game Six in Washington to even the 1924 World Series at three games apiece.*

Opposite bottom: *Washington's Goose Goslin is thrown out at first on an outstanding play by shortstop Travis Jackson in the second inning of the '24 Series opener. Giant first baseman Bill Terry takes the throw. The Giants won 4-3.*

Above: *Washington pitcher Walter Johnson with a Salvation Army volunteer. The popular Big Train got his first postseason victory in the World Series finale.*

Upper right: *Washington manager Bucky Harris played second, hit .333 and outmanaged the Giants' incomparable John McGraw in the Series. "Boy Wonder" Harris became the youngest manager to win a World Series.*

Lower right: *The Senators' Joe Judge slides home with the winning run after Earl McNeely's hit took a bad hop over third baseman Fred Lindstrom's head in the twelfth inning of Game Seven.*

YOU COULD LOOK IT UP
The 1927 Yankees

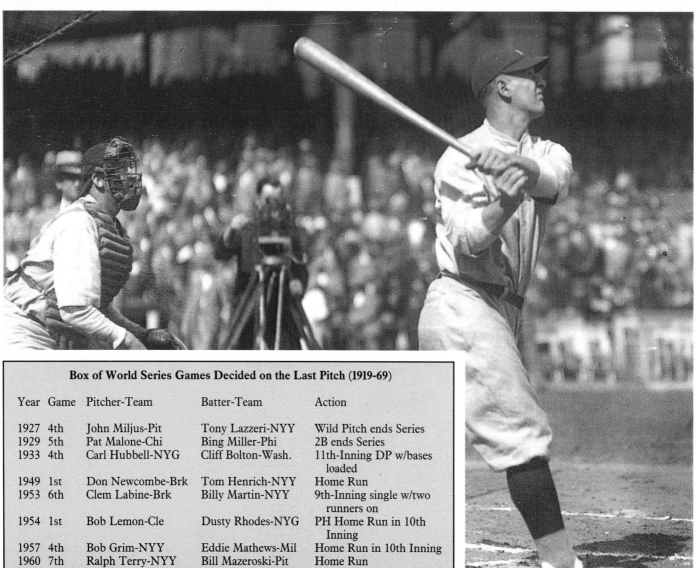

Box of World Series Games Decided on the Last Pitch (1919-69)

Year	Game	Pitcher-Team	Batter-Team	Action
1927	4th	John Miljus-Pit	Tony Lazzeri-NYY	Wild Pitch ends Series
1929	5th	Pat Malone-Chi	Bing Miller-Phi	2B ends Series
1933	4th	Carl Hubbell-NYG	Cliff Bolton-Wash.	11th-Inning DP w/bases loaded
1949	1st	Don Newcombe-Brk	Tom Henrich-NYY	Home Run
1953	6th	Clem Labine-Brk	Billy Martin-NYY	9th-Inning single w/two runners on
1954	1st	Bob Lemon-Cle	Dusty Rhodes-NYG	PH Home Run in 10th Inning
1957	4th	Bob Grim-NYY	Eddie Mathews-Mil	Home Run in 10th Inning
1960	7th	Ralph Terry-NYY	Bill Mazeroski-Pit	Home Run
1962	7th	Ralph Terry-NYY	Willie McCovey-SF	Line out w/two runners on
1964	3rd	Barney Schultz-St.L	Mickey Mantle-NYY	Home Run
1969	4th	Pete Richert-Bal	J.C. Martin-NYM	Sac Bunt and Error

Opposite top: *The 1927 Yankees, widely regarded as the greatest team in baseball history. New York went 110-44 to win the pennant by 19 games, then swept the Pittsburgh Pirates in a four-game Series. The Yanks stayed in first place all season, and led the league in runs, triples, home runs, batting average, slugging average, earned run average, shutouts, fewest bases on balls and fewest runs allowed.*

Opposite bottom: *Not to be overshadowed by Babe Ruth's 60 homers, Lou Gehrig hit .373, with 52 doubles, 47 homers and 175 runs batted in.*

Left top: *Herb Pennock won 19 games for the '27 Yankees and another big one in the Series. A dandy curveballer and control specialist, he was 5-0 overall in postseason play.*

Left: *Yankee manager Miller Huggins. The Mighty Mite never loomed as large as in 1927, but he also won six pennants in eight years (1921-28) and disciplined the boisterous Babe when he needed it.*

Pages 48-49: *Some '27 Yankees who together homered 121 times and drove in 506 runs. From left: Earle Combs, Bob Meusel, Lou Gehrig, Babe Ruth.*

1927 Yankees' Stats Compared to the League and Other Great Teams

	Team	HRs	League	%	Runs	League	%
1927	Yankees	158	439	36	975	6094	16
1936	Yankees	182	758	24	1065	7009	15
1944	Cardinals	100	575	17	772	5295	15
1953	Dodgers	208	1197	17	955	5914	16
1961	Yankees	240	1534	16	827	7342	11
1963	Dodgers	110	1215	9	640	6181	10
1966	Orioles	175	1365	13	755	6276	12

NEGRO LEAGUES IN THE TWENTIES

Negro Leagues Batting Champs

Year	Negro National League		Eastern Colored League	
1920	Cris. Torriente	.411	did not play	
1921	Charles Blackwell	.448	did not play	
1922	Heavy Johnson	.389	did not play	
1923	Cris. Torriente	.412	Jud Wilson	.373
1924	Dobie Moore	.453	Pop Lloyd	.433
1925	Edgar Wesley	.416	Oscar Charleston	.445
1926	Mule Suttles	.418	Robert Hudspeth	.365
1927	Red Parnell	.426	Clarence Jenkins	.398
1928	Pythian Russ	.406	Pop Lloyd	.564

CLARK
(BALTIMORE)

GIBSON
(GRAYS)

Opposite left: *John Henry "Pop" Lloyd was the greatest shortstop in the Negro leagues – and more. "You could put [Honus] Wagner and Lloyd in a bag together, and whichever you pulled out, you couldn't go wrong," Connie Mack once said.*

Opposite top right: *A steady, dependable third baseman and a scientific spray hitter, William "Judy" Johnson played in the Negro leagues from 1921 to 1938.*

Opposite bottom right: *First a pitcher, then a manager, finally an owner and executive, Andrew "Rube" Foster was the first president of the Negro National League.*

Left: *For hitting homers as far as 575 feet and as often as 75 times a season, Josh Gibson was called "the black Babe Ruth." An outstanding catcher in 1930-46, he could just as easily have been called "the black Bill Dickey."*

Below: *The Kansas City Monarchs (shown here in 1936) were probably the all-time great Negro National League team, and won the first Negro World Series in 1924.*

KANSAS CITY MONARCH
WORLDS COLORED CHAMPIONS
BASE BALL CLUB

Right: *It is said that James "Cool Papa" Bell could turn off the switch and hop into bed before the light went out. That could be a tall tale, though Bell said the light had a delay-causing short in it. It's verifiably true that Bell scored from second on a fly against Dizzy Dean and from first on a sacrifice bunt against Bob Lemon – the latter a pretty fair feat for a 45-year-old. Called Cool Papa for his calm demeanor, he was a blazing fast runner who stole 175 bases in a 200-game season and circled the bases in 12 seconds flat, easily bettering the major-league record. Bell played from 1922 to 1946, mostly with the Homestead Grays.*

Good enough to bat .392 against white big leaguers, the switch-hitting outfielder was too old to play in the majors when they integrated, but compassionate enough to help other, younger blacks make the transition. He counseled Jackie Robinson to switch from short to second, where he settled with the Dodgers. Bell sat out the final doubleheader of the 1946 season so that Monte Irvin could win the batting title and boost his chances to be drafted. Robinson and Irvin not only made the majors but the Hall of Fame.

DECADE HIGHLIGHTS

Decade Leaders, 1920-29

	National League		American League	
Batting				
BA	Rogers Hornsby	.382	Harry Heilmann	.364
HRs	Rogers Hornsby	250	Babe Ruth	467
RBIs	Rogers Hornsby	1153	Babe Ruth	1330
Hits	Rogers Hornsby	2085	Sam Rice	2010
Runs	Rogers Hornsby	1195	Babe Ruth	1365
2B	Rogers Hornsby	405	Tris Speaker	398
BB	Rogers Hornsby	753	Babe Ruth	1236
SB	Max Carey	346	Sam Rice	254
Pitching				
Wins	Burleigh Grimes	190	Herb Pennock	162
ERA	Dazzy Vance	3.10	Urban Shocker	3.33
SO	Dazzy Vance	1464	Bob Shawkey	788
IP	Burleigh Grimes	2798	Waite Hoyt	2346

Opposite: *In 1922 George Sisler (left, with admiring rival Eddie Collins) led the American League with a .420 average, 246 hits, 134 runs, 51 stolen bases and 18 triples. Oh, yes: He also had 42 doubles and drove in 105 runs.*

Right: *In the 10 years of the '20s, Rogers Hornsby won seven batting titles, and led the league nine times in slugging average, eight times in on-base percentage, five times in runs, four times in hits, four times in doubles, twice in homers and once in triples. The abrasive Rajah also played for four teams during that time.*

Below: *The incomparable 1927 Yankees boasted batting leaders in every important offensive category but average, and pitching pacesetters in winning percentage, saves and fewest hits per game.*

Pages 56-57: *Who was better? It hardly mattered: Babe Ruth and Lou Gehrig were baseball in the '20s.*

During the Depression baseball didn't suffer as much as other industries. Not a single stadium closed. No franchises folded. Nary a player was laid off. The fans actually benefited, because the game became pleasantly viewer-friendly during the 1930s.

This is not to say that baseball totally escaped hard times. Attendance slipped badly after the 1930 season; the St. Louis Browns, to cite the most extreme example, drew 1.2 million fans during the entire decade. Players took salary cuts when teams began losing money. After winning pennants in 1929-31, Connie Mack, the financially pressed owner-manager of the Philadelphia Athletics, sold off his best players. The A's fell to last in 1935 and were never the same again. In perhaps the worst trade ever, Washington owner Clark Griffith sold his star son-in-law, player-manager Joe Cronin, to the Red Sox for a shortstop and $250,000. The Senators were never the same again, either.

As a sign of the times, baseball strategists slept through the innovation-empty decade. In the spirit of the times, the players began throwing unusually nasty nicknames at one another: Stinky, Goofy, Blimp, Fatty, to name just a few. Even the atmosphere at games was altered. "People avoided eye contact," said Fred Lindstrom, the old Giant infielder. "That's one of the things I remember. It was like everybody had his own thoughts and was in deep concentration upon them; or maybe it was that people were so self-conscious of their problems they were ashamed to look at one another. And at the ballpark the cheering sounded forced, like it was expected of them rather than spontaneous, as it had always been."

Nonetheless, baseball functioned as a kind of never-never land for a society in shambles. In 1930, the first full year of the Depression, the National League juiced up the baseball, both leagues lowered the height of the stitches to make balls tougher to grip, and the batters went gaga. While the Americans batted .288, the Nationals hit a whopping .303, the Giants' Bill Terry became the last NL player to clear .400 (.401) and the Cubs' Hack Wilson set an all-time standard by driving in 190 runs. The St. Louis Cardinals, a 53-52 fourth-place team 13½ games out on August 8, went 39-10 to take the NL pennant in the decade's best race. Gratitude from the stands? You bet. Even as their pockets began emptying out, the fans set an all-time record: 10.1 million of them crowded into the parks, a mark that wouldn't be topped until 1945.

When the NL raised the stitches on their baseballs in 1931, league runs dropped 13 percent and major-league attendance plummeted 38 percent. But the crowds kept getting their money's worth. The seven-game 1931 Series, staged by Pepper Martin, Jimmie Foxx, the champion Cardinals and the Athletics, was probably the decade's best. In the 1932 Series, Babe Ruth either did or didn't point to center field before hitting his "called-shot" homer off the Cubs' Charlie Root; it didn't matter, because he created an unforgettably theatrical scene with his gestures. Some observers have called it the greatest moment in baseball history.

It was an era of character. There was Lou Gehrig "giving the nation continuity from past strength through the dark times to the day of renewed vigor," according to historian Donald Honig. Jewish slugger Hank Greenberg qualified as an early-day Jackie Robinson for thriving in the face of ethnic slurs. Joe DiMaggio simply defined grace and style. It was an era of characters. "He's an unusual hitter," Dodger manager Casey Stengel said

of the Cubs' Billy Herman. "Sometimes he stands straight up, and sometimes his head is so close to the plate he looks like John the Baptist." Dizzy Dean, clown prince of the Cardinals' Gas House Gang, dropped quite a few verbal gems of his own. "If you say you're going to do it, and you go out and do it, it ain't braggin'," he said. The Arkansas-born son of a cotton sharecropper, Dean would drop by the office of team executive Branch Rickey to "talk country." Said Rickey: "If there was more like him, I'd get out of the game." But people went to the games just to see Dean, who could pitch as well as he could talk.

No thirties team won more games and world championships than the Yankees – 970 and 5. The Yankees' recruiting dragnet reached far and wide – to California, where they mined the richest new mother lode available, and to the Italian-American community (Joe DiMaggio, Frankie Crosetti), the hottest new immigrant player pool. The Series winners that the Yankees fielded in 1936-39 may have been their greatest sustained showing of strength. But the whole game was better than ever. Was there a more poetic baseball expression than "homer in the gloamin'" – the night-shrouded dinger Gabby Hartnett cracked to put the pennant-bound '38

Cubs in first? The bitterest Yankee haters could take solace in the late-decade coming of world-class players like Cleveland's Bob Feller and Boston's Ted Williams.

The fans were getting their money's worth, all right. In 1930 fans were allowed to keep foul balls instead of throwing them back on the field. Uniform numbers became standard practice in 1932, the All-Star game commenced a year later, and night ball began serving the working multitudes on May 24, 1935, in Cincinnati. The Hall of Fame opened in 1939, even as television captured its first big-league game. Symbolic of better times ahead, the term "base ball" became one word.

The industry as a whole actually made money during the decade. But you had to figure the players enjoyed the Depression more than anyone else involved with the pastime. ". . .sometimes we'd forget there was a real world out there," said Hall of Famer Lloyd Waner. "Remember, we went from the hotel to the ballpark, back to the hotel, and then onto the train for the next go-around. All of our reservations were made for us, all of our meals were paid for. Did that for six months. Then the season would be over and my brother Paul and me would go back to Oklahoma, and then we would realize how bad things were."

THE YEAR OF THE HITTER – 1930

Above left: *The last National Leaguer to clear .400, the Giants' Bill Terry hit .401 in 1930.*

Above: *First a Yankee pitcher, then a more successful NL outfielder, Lefty O'Doul hit .349 over 11 seasons. In 1930 he hit .383 for the Phillies.*

Left: *One of the greatest sluggers in NL history, the Phillies' Chuck Klein averaged 36 homers, 139 RBIs, 131 runs and 229 hits in 1929-33. In 1930 the rightfielder had 40 homers and a record 44 assists.*

Opposite: *The only player with more than 150 RBIs for two straight years – 157 in 1929 and 190 in 1930 – the 5' 6", 210-pound Hack Wilson got his nickname because he resembled Russian wrestler George Hackenschmidt.*

REBORN GIANTS OF THE THIRTIES

Opposite top: *The Giants' manager Bill Terry conducts a rookie-school class in Baton Rouge, Louisiana before the 1938 season. Weeded out of 180 registrants, all five players reported to the minor leagues and languished there.*

Opposite bottom: *Pitcher Hal Schumacher gets back to first safely after hitting a two-run single in the fifth game of the 1933 World Series. Prince Hal's Giants won 4-3 in 10 innings to wrap up the Series.*

Right: *Mel Ott scoring in the 1933 Series. The Giants' rightfielder led both teams by batting .389, with two homers and four RBIs.*

Below: *Another Giant Hall of Famer, Carl Hubbell warms up for a campaign. Hubbell won 253 times despite relying on the oft-debilitating screwball.*

BEST YANKEES EVER?
Five Great Yankees of the Decade

Right: *Babe Ruth takes Lou Gehrig's picture before the 1932 opener at Shibe Park. When the game started, Ruth became the focus. He homered twice while the Yankees beat the A's 12-6.*

Below: *Joe McCarthy managed the Yankees to eight pennants and seven world titles in the 1930s and 1940s.*

Below right: *"Poosh-'Em Up" Tony Lazzeri was not only a stalwart Yankee second baseman in 1926-36 but a notable run producer. He drove in more than 100 seven times.*

Opposite: *The Yankees never seemed to run out of young sensations. Here Joe DiMaggio (left), star freshman of the '36 class, sits with '37 newcomer Tommy Henrich.*

A TOUGH TIME FOR PITCHERS
Best Pitchers of the Decade

Opposite top: *Though he didn't reach the majors until he was 25, Lefty Grove won 300 games for the Athletics (1925-33) and Red Sox (1934-41) and allowed only 3.06 earned runs per game in a lively-ball era. Grove was known for his temper (he trashed a clubhouse when a teammate's error cost him a record 17th straight win), less for his generosity (he awarded all of his 300 game balls to kid leagues).*

Opposite lower left: *When a 17-year-old Bob Feller fanned eight Cardinals in a three-inning exhibition stint, people figured he might be the real thing. "He showed me more speed than I have ever seen from an American League pitcher," said umpire Red Ormsby, "and I don't except Walter Johnson." Ormsby's description was anything but hyperbolic. Despite missing almost four seasons during World War II, the powerful Iowa farm kid – he had beefed up by carrying 2,000 gallons of water a day – won 266 games and threw three no-hitters.*

Opposite lower right: *Giant pitcher Carl Hubbell in 1934, when he led the league in both complete games (25) and saves (8).*

Right: *Feller's best pitches were his fastball and curve, but he somehow had time to develop a slider while winning five campaign ribbons and eight battle stars as gun-crew chief on the battleship* Alabama. *Feller returned from the war and promptly threw a no-hitter at Yankee Stadium. "That," he said, "was my most satisfying victory."*

Above: *Pat Malone kisses Yankee teammate Lefty Gomez to congratulate him for his 4-2 win over the Giants in the final game of the 1937 World Series. The Series took only five games, no surprise for either the winners, who had won the pennant by 13, or Gomez, who had led the AL with 21 wins.*

Left: *Gomez and rival pitcher Junior Thompson before the 1939 World Series. The Yankees won their fourth straight Series, this one in four games, to conclude perhaps their most dominant era.*

Opposite: *Johnny Vander Meer pitched a record two straight no-hitters for the '38 Reds.*

BIG POISON AND LITTLE POISON
The Waner Brothers

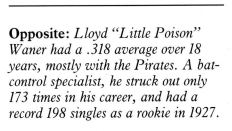

Opposite: *Lloyd "Little Poison" Waner had a .318 average over 18 years, mostly with the Pirates. A bat-control specialist, he struck out only 173 times in his career, and had a record 198 singles as a rookie in 1927.*

Above right: *Rookie Lloyd (left) and one-year veteran Paul (third from left) shake hands with Babe Ruth and Lou Gehrig before the 1927 World Series. This would be their only postseason trip in the Waner brothers' long careers.*

Right: *Paul "Big Poison" Waner won three batting titles, had 200 or more hits eight times and hit .333 for 20 seasons. According to legend, Paul was given his 3,000th hit on a grounder off an infielder's glove. Preferring to wait for a clean hit, he supposedly signaled to the official scorer to charge an error – and got his wish.*

CONNIE'S COMEBACK
Connie Mack's Athletics of the Early Thirties

Left: *Connie Mack managed major league teams longer (53 years), won more games (3,776) and lost more (4,025) than any skipper in baseball history. Handling the Philadelphia Athletics in 1901-50, he built powerhouse teams that won three pennants in 1910-14 and three more in 1929-31. The Tall Tactician made a striking figure sitting in the dugout in a suit and straw hat and directing the team with a rolled-up program. With a keen eye for talent, he acquired stars like Frank "Home Run" Baker, Eddie Collins, Lefty Grove, Jimmie Foxx, Mickey Cochrane and Al Simmons. Mack's undoing was his stubborn pride. He broke up the first winner by refusing to raise salaries in competition with the upstart Federal League; and the second mini-dynasty when he claimed financial stress during the Depression.*

Opposite top: *Jimmie Foxx is congratulated after homering in Game Four of the 1931 World Series. The A's beat the Cardinals 3-0.*

Opposite bottom left: *George Earnshaw won 24, 22 and 21 games for the 1929-31 A's, and had a 1.58 ERA in the World Series.*

Opposite bottom right: *The A's Al Simmons was known as Bucketfoot Al, but he must have been doing something right at the plate. The righthanded-hitting American League outfielder batted with his left foot aimed at third base, but he had six 200-hit seasons, 307 homers and a .334 lifetime average. In Game Four of the 1929 Series he started a 10-run seventh-inning rally that overcame an 8-0 deficit by homering off the Cubs' Charlie Root, then singled to set up the ninth run and scored the 10th himself.*

Years	Manager	Team	Year	Next Team	Year
	Managers With the Most Years Between Pennants (1919-1969)				
22	Bucky Harris	Senators	1925	Yankees	1947
15	Connie Mack	Athletics	1914	Athletics	1929
15	Hugh Jennings	Tigers	1909	Giants	1924*
13	Joe Cronin	Senators	1933	Red Sox	1946
12	Al Dark	Giants	1962	Athletics	1974
11	Bill McKechnie	Cardinals	1928	Reds	1939
10	Leo Durocher	Dodgers	1941	Giants	1951
10	Charlie Grimm	Cubs	1935	Cubs	1945**

Managed 44 games in McGraw's absence during 1924.
**Fired in 1938 with the Cubs in third place. They eventually won the pennant.*

HARD TIMES
The Depression's Impact on Baseball

Opposite top left: *A stylized drawing of Babe Ruth's "called-shot" homer in the 1932 World Series. With the score tied 4-4 in the sixth inning of Game Three, Ruth supposedly pointed to a spot in deep center field at the base of the flagpole where he claimed he would homer, then did it on the next pitch from Cub pitcher Charlie Root.*

Opposite top right: *The Senators' owner Clark Griffith (shown as a manager in younger days) traded his son-in-law and star shortstop Joe Cronin after winning a pennant in 1934 for a shortstop and $250,000. The Senators were never the same again, prompting the later refrain, "First in war, first in peace, and last in the American League."*

Opposite below: *A smiling President Herbert Hoover throws out the first pitch to open the 1929 season. Depression awaited him.*

Above: *Ossie Bluege of the Senators dives safely back to third while Giant third baseman Travis Jackson applies a late tag in Game Three of the 1933 Series. The Senators won 4-0, but the Giants took the Series in five games.*

Above right: *This shot of Athletic teammates waiting to greet Jimmie Foxx after a three-run homer depicts blank uniform backs. The Yankees first put numbers on their uniforms in 1929, and other teams quickly followed suit in the early 1930s.*

High and Low Franchise Attendance During the 1930s							
Franchise	League	Year	High	Finish	Year	Low	Finish
Boston	NL	1933	517,803	4th	1935	232,754	8th
Brooklyn	NL	1930	1,097,339	4th	1934	434,188	6th
Chicago	NL	1930	1,463,624	2nd	1933	594,112	3rd
Cincinnati	NL	1939	981,443	1st	1934	206,773	8th
New York	NL	1937	926,887	1st	1932	484,868	6th
Philadelphia	NL	1930	299,007	8th	1933	156,421	7th
Pittsburgh	NL	1938	641,033	2nd	1931	260,392	5th
St. Louis	NL	1931	608,535	1st	1933	256,171	5th
Boston	AL	1938	646,459	2nd	1932	182,150	8th
Chicago	AL	1939	594,104	4th	1932	233,198	7th
Cleveland	AL	1938	652,006	3rd	1933	387,936	4th
Detroit	AL	1937	1,072,276	2nd	1933	320,972	5th
New York	AL	1930	1,169,230	3rd	1935	657,508	2nd
Philadelphia	AL	1930	721,663	1st	1935	233,173	8th
St. Louis	AL	1931	179,126	5th	1935	80,922	7th
Washington	AL	1930	614,474	2nd	1936	255,011	4th

THE STARS COME OUT
The Beginning of the All-Star Game

Above: *The American League All-Star team poses before the first midseason tilt, played at Chicago's Comiskey Park in 1933. The All-Star game idea originated with Arch Ward, sports editor of the Chicago Tribune.*

Right: *Jimmy Dykes scores with the AL's first All-Star run.*

Opposite top: *The Phillies' Chuck Klein bats for the National League in the first inning of the '33 midseason classic. Boston's Rick Ferrell is catching. The AL won 4-2 when Lefty Gomez got both the victory and first RBI and Yankee teammate Babe Ruth, a spry 38, clouted a two-run homer.*

Opposite bottom: *Carl Hubbell (left) and Lefty Grove share a moment before the first All-Star game. In the second All-Star game Hubbell struck out a record five consecutive American Leaguers – Babe Ruth, Lou Gehrig, Jimmie Foxx, Al Simmons and Joe Cronin.*

NIGHT BALL LIGHTS UP THE DEPRESSION

Left: *In 1938 Cincy's Johnny Vander Meer pitched his record second straight no-hitter in the first night game ever played at Ebbets Field.*

Above: *Cincinnati's dynamic executive Larry S. MacPhail championed night baseball. In three years with the Reds and five with Brooklyn, he pioneered two innovations that affected baseball forever – night games and radio broadcasts. MacPhail was elected to the Hall of Fame for his important contributions to major league baseball.*

Opposite top: *The Reds and visiting Phillies play major league baseball's first night game on May 24, 1935 before a capacity crowd at Crosley Field. Franklin D. Roosevelt himself pushed a button that turned on 632 lights before the historic game.*

Opposite bottom: *The first night game played at Ebbets Field was held on June 15, 1938, between the Brooklyn Dodgers and the Cincinnati Reds. The Dodgers were no-hit in the game by Johnny Vander Meer, 6-0, for his unprecedented second straight no-hitter. Larry MacPhail, now running the Dodgers, had arranged pre-game festivities featuring Olympic track star Jesse Owens and baseball immortal Babe Ruth.*

Sites of First Night Games by Franchise

Team-League	Date	Opponent	Outcome		Attendance
Cincinnati-NL	5-24-35	Philadelphia	Won	2-1	20,422
Brooklyn-NL	6-15-38	Cincinnati	Lost	6-0	38,748
Philadelphia-AL	5-16-39	Cleveland	Won	8-3	15,109
Philadelphia-NL	6-01-39	Pittsburgh	Lost	5-2	8,000
Cleveland-AL	6-27-39	Detroit	Won	5-0	55,307
Chicago-AL	8-14-39	St. Louis	Won	5-2	30,000
New York-NL	5-24-40	Boston	Won	8-1	22,260
St. Louis-AL	5-24-40	Cleveland	Lost	3-2	25,562
St. Louis-NL	6-04-40	Brooklyn	Lost	10-1	23,500
Pittsburgh-NL	6-04-40	Boston	Won	14-2	20,319
Washington-AL	5-28-41	New York	Lost	6-5	25,000
Boston-NL	5-11-46	New York	Lost	5-1	35,945
New York-AL	5-28-46	Washington	Lost	2-1	48,895
Boston-AL	6-13-47	Chicago	Won	5-3	34,510
Detroit-AL	6-15-48	Chicago	Won	4-1	54,480

CHARACTERS
Mavericks of the Thirties

Opposite top: *The Cardinals' Gas House Gang – here featuring Pepper Martin (left), mascot Yoyo and Rip Collins – could ham it up without losing their winning touch.*

Opposite bottom: *The Cardinals' starting lineup for the 1934 World Series opener. From left: Dizzy Dean, pitcher; Leo Durocher, shortstop; Ernie Orsatti, center field; Bill DeLancey, catcher; Rip Collins, first base; Joe Medwick, left field; manager Frankie Frisch, second base; Jack Rothrock, right field; Pepper Martin, third base.*

Right: *Ol' Diz played the tuba and had the Tigers' tune as well: He went 2-1, with a 1.73 ERA, and pitched a six-hit shutout in the '34 Series finale after only one day of rest.*

Page 84: *Pepper Martin could play several instruments and had a lyrical playing style, too. The Wild Horse of the Osage led the National League in stolen bases three times and runs once.*

Page 85: *Rough-tough Cardinal outfielder Joe "Ducky" Medwick won the 1937 Triple Crown with a .374 average, 31 homers and 154 RBIs. His nickname, which he despised, came from his duck-like waddle. His hard-nosed philosophy was "base hits and bucks." The only player ever to be benched for safety reasons, Medwick left the 1934 Series finale on Commissioner Landis's orders after Detroit fans pelted him with garbage in retaliation for his hard slide into Tiger third baseman Marv Owen.*

CHARACTER
Players of Integrity

Opposite top: *While the 1935 Tigers gun for a second straight pennant, pitcher Firpo Marberry checks out his infield. From left: Charlie Gehringer, second base; Bill Rogell, shortstop; Hank Greenberg, first base, and Marv Owen, third base. Gehringer and Greenberg were especially stolid performers. Helping the Tigers repeat, "Mechanical Man" Gehringer routinely batted .330 and Greenberg had a league-leading 36 homers and 170 RBIs.*

Opposite bottom: *Lou Gehrig and Babe Ruth, who had long feuded, embraced on Lou Gehrig Day: July 4, 1939. Gehrig, dying of a spinal disease that would be named after him, was one of the most popular players in baseball history.*

Right: *Cub catcher Gabby Hartnett hit the darkness-shrouded "homer in the gloamin'" for the '38 flag.*

Below: *Hank Greenberg was a role model supreme. Traded by the Tigers late in his career, he helped turn Ralph Kiner into a Hall-of-Fame slugger with his advice and example.*

MR. VERSATILITY – JOE CRONIN

Opposite: *In 1933 life was relatively simple for Joe Cronin. He was merely the pennant-winning manager, shortstop and star of the Washington Senators.*

Left: *By 1941 he was managing the Red Sox and Ted Williams.*

Below: *As a slugger and shortstop, Cronin was a legendary two-way performer. Here he forces the Giants' Kiddo Davis and throws to first for a double play in Game Five of the 1933 World Series.*

Page 90-91: *In 1936 shortstop-manager Cronin warms up for a season with the Red Sox. A legendary run producer, Cronin was the only shortstop with four 100-run, 100-RBI seasons.*

Page 91 inset: *In 1958 Cronin, now the Red Sox general manager, was about to be named American League president. Overall, he spent half a century in major league baseball.*

THE HALL OF FAME OPENS

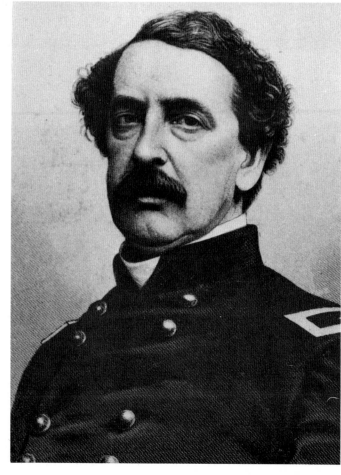

The First Hall of Fame Inductees (1936-1939)

Member	Years	Position	Induction
Ty Cobb	1905-1928	Outfield	1936
Babe Ruth	1914-1935	Outfield	1936
Walter Johnson	1907-1927	Pitcher	1936
Christy Mathewson	1900-1916	Pitcher	1936
Honus Wagner	1897-1917	Shortstop	1936
Nap Lajoie	1896-1916	Second Base	1937
Tris Speaker	1907-1928	Outfield	1937
Cy Young	1890-1911	Pitcher	1937
Grover Alexander	1911-1930	Pitcher	1938
George Sisler	1915-1930	First Base	1939
Eddie Collins	1906-1930	Second Base	1939
Willie Keeler	1892-1910	Outfield	1939
Cap Anson	1871-1897	First Base	1939
Candy Cummings	1872-1877	Pitcher	1939
Buck Ewing	1880-1897	Catcher	1939
Old Hoss Radbourn	1880-1891	Pitcher	1939
Al Spalding	1871-1878	Pitcher-Exec	1939
Lou Gehrig	1923-1939	First Base	1939

Non-playing Personnel

Member	Position	Induction
George Wright	Manager	1937
Ban Johnson	Executive	1937
Connie Mack	Manager	1937
Morgan Bulkeley	Executive	1937
John McGraw	Manager	1937
Alex. Cartwright	Executive	1938
Henry Chadwick	Writer	1938
Charles Comiskey	Manager	1939

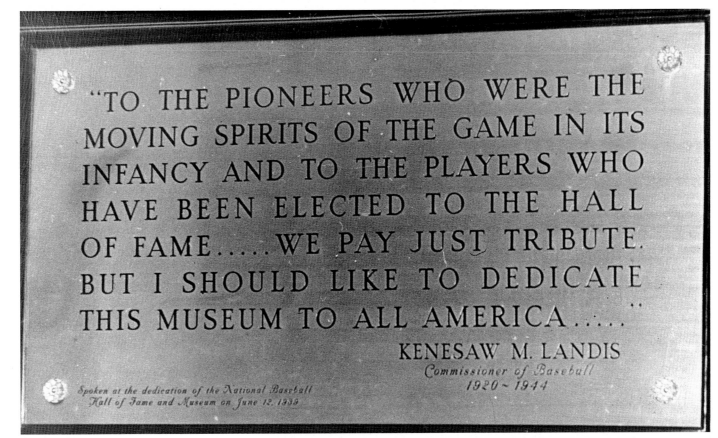

Opposite top: *Joe DiMaggio checked out his likeness the 1955 day he was installed as a Cooperstown immortal. DiMaggio has also been voted baseball's greatest living player.*

Opposite bottom: *Abner Doubleday, the Union soldier once thought to have invented baseball at Cooperstown, New York, in 1839. Doubleday's role has since been disproved, but the Hall opened in the picture-postcard town on the 100th anniversary of his "invention."*

Above: *A plaque in Cooperstown bears words from Commissioner Landis's Hall of Fame dedication speech. Originally intended as a baseball centennial celebration at Doubleday Field by Cooperstown locals, the event gained momentum when Landis and NL President Ford Frick convinced the Baseball Writers Association of America to cast votes to pick the all-time greatest to be honored in the Hall of Fame. Elections began in 1936, but the Hall itself was not dedicated until 1939.*

Right: *The Great Moments Room in the Hall of Fame.*

Left: *Some of the first Hall of Fame inductees attend the 1939 opening. Front row, from left: Eddie Collins, Babe Ruth, Connie Mack, Cy Young. Top: Honus Wagner, Grover Cleveland Alexander, Tris Speaker, Nap Lajoie, George Sisler, Walter Johnson. Ty Cobb was delayed en route from California and arrived moments after the photo was taken.*

TERRORS AT THE TURN
Players Making their Marks in the Late Thirties

Left: *Bob Feller went 17-11 in 1938, his first year as a fulltime starter. "Feller is the best pitcher living," Ted Williams said three years later. "I don't think anyone is ever going to throw a ball faster than he does. And his curve isn't human."*

Below left: *The Senators' prime-cut first baseman, Mickey Vernon, broke in during the 1939 season and stayed for four decades and 2,495 hits.*

Below: *Indian third baseman Ken Keltner, better known for making two dazzling backhanded stops to end Joe DiMaggio's record 56-game hitting streak in 1941, could bat pretty well himself. In 1939, only his second full season, he had 191 hits.*

Opposite: *"Where do you get all that power?" Red Sox teammate Jimmie Foxx asks Ted Williams. As a lean rookie in 1939, The Kid hit .327, with 31 homers and 145 RBIs.*

FORGOTTEN FIELDERS

Above: *The Phillies' Chuck Klein receives his 1932 Most Valuable Player Award. In addition to hitting .348 that year, with 38 homers, 20 stolen bases and 137 RBIs, he played a solid right field.*

Left: *Giant shortstop Dick Bartell scores in the 1937 World Series. In 1936 Rowdy Richard hit .296 and led all shortstops in assists, total chances and double plays.*

Opposite: *A pre-Keltner Cleveland third baseman, Willie Kamm, slides into his favorite bag against Rogers Hornsby in 1934. Kamm led the AL in fielding percentage eight times and was consistently among the pacesetters in every category but errors.*

BEST OF THE BACKSTOPS

Opposite: *A National League catcher for Brooklyn and Boston during the thirties, Al Lopez held the all-time record for games caught (1918) until Bob Boone broke it in 1987.*

Above: *The Yankees' Bill Dickey was a record-setting catcher, as his 13 straight seasons catching at least 100 games, and his .362 average in 1936, attest.*

Above right: *One of baseball's greatest hitting catchers, Ernie Lombardi led the NL in batting twice, including during his 1938 MVP year, when he hit .342 for the Reds.*

Right: *Mickey Cochrane dives for the tag. Cochrane caught for five pennant winners in a seven-season run (1929-35) with the Athletics and Tigers.*

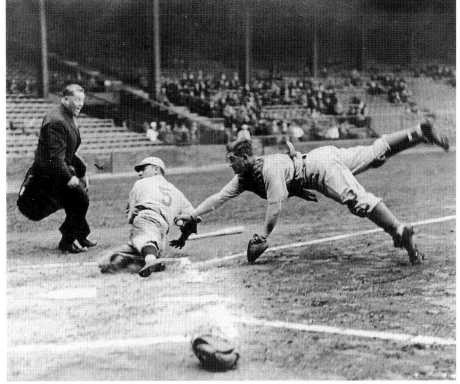

DECADE HIGHLIGHTS

Decade Leaders, 1930-39

	National League		American League	
Batting				
BA	Bill Terry	.351	Lou Gehrig	.343
HRs	Mel Ott	308	Jimmie Foxx	415
RBIs	Mel Ott	1135	Jimmie Foxx	1403
Hits	Chuck Klein	1676	Charlie Gehringer	1865
Runs	Mel Ott	1095	Lou Gehrig	1257
2B	Joe Medwick	353	Charlie Gehringer	400
BB	Mel Ott	956	Lou Gehrig	1028
Pitching				
Wins	Carl Hubbell	188	Lefty Grove	199
ERA	Carl Hubbell	2.71	Lefty Grove	2.91
SO	Carl Hubbell	1282	Lefty Gomez	1337
IP	Carl Hubbell	2596	Red Ruffing	2439

Opposite: *Cub catcher/manager Gabby Hartnett is mobbed after his "homer in the gloamin'" put the '38 Cubs in first to stay. With his powerful arm and take-charge attitude, Hartnett rates as one of the NL's all-time greatest catchers.*

Above: *The Giants' Carl Hubbell (left) and the Yankees' Irving "Bump" Hadley pose before meeting in the fourth game of the 1937 Series. Hubbell won 7-3, but that was the Giants' only consolation in a five-game Series loss.*

Right: *In 1936, Hadley (left) and third baseman Red Rolfe take movies of teammate Joe DiMaggio before another Yankees-Giants Series. The Yankees won in six, with DiMag hitting .346.*

Page 104: *Cub slugger Hack Wilson was considered the National League's Babe Ruth in his heyday.*

Page 105: *A slugging catcher and first baseman, part-Cherokee Rudy York had four 30-homer seasons and six 100-RBI years for the Tigers and Red Sox. Working for the Yankees after his playing days, he may have been the first advance scout in baseball.*

The 1940s were easily this century's most spectacular decade – in baseball as well as in world history. The forties began with our national pastime played almost exclusively by whites, mostly in daylight, and followed mainly by spectators, listeners and viewers in their own communities. When the decade ended, the game was played by people of all races, increasingly at night, and followed on radio and television by millions from coast to coast. In between were two pennant races ending in dead heats and requiring playoffs, the most unforgettable season ever, and a strange and misunderstood wartime interlude. Almost forgotten in the frenzy, the Dodgers emerged as a national power – an America's team before the hype of cable TV.

The 1940 season was unusual enough for a whole decade. In the American League a Detroit pitcher named Floyd Giebell beat Cleveland's Bob Feller on the final Saturday of the season to clinch the pennant. It was Giebell's last big-league win. For their part, the Indians had been lucky to remain in contention that long: all 25 players signed a petition unsuccessfully demanding the firing of unpopular manager Ossie Vitt. In the National League the pennant-winning Cincinnati Reds found themselves with unprecedented catching problems when future Hall-of-Famer Ernie Lombardi was injured and his replacement, Willard Hershberger, grew despondent over a poor performance and committed suicide in a

hotel room. The solution: activate 40-year-old coach Jimmy Wilson for the World Series. The result: Wilson hit .353 and helped the Reds win their first world championship in 21 years.

Then came the nonpareil 1941 season, best chronicled in Robert W. Creamer's *Baseball in '41*. It was the year that Ted Williams had the game's last .400 season while winning the All-Star game with a dramatic home run, and Joe DiMaggio hit safely in a record 56 straight games. What wonderful characters and spectacular contrasts they were! The obsessive Williams, who thought only about hitting when he was awake, had a postal scale in the clubhouse to weigh his bats. When a Louisville Slugger official challenged him to decide by feel which of six bats was half an ounce heavier than the others, he did. Teddy Ballgame needed no help from anyone. On the last day of the season he approached a doubleheader batting .3996, which would have rounded off to .400. The end of daylight savings the previous day sent autumn shadows cascading across the field. Declining to sit out that perilous afternoon, Williams went 6-for-8 in Philadelphia's Shibe Park to finish at .406.

DiMaggio's was the more popular quest. In the 38th game of his streak he was hitless in the eighth inning of a home game the Yankees were leading 3-1. DiMag was scheduled to bat fourth if at all. With a man on and one out, Tommy Henrich came to the plate fearing a streak-

Pages 106-7: *Mel Ott, manager and Hall-of-Fame slugger for the New York Giants, takes a cut in a game with the Dodgers in 1945.*

Opposite: *Five Yankees were selected to the 1949 American League All-Star team. From left: Vic Raschi, pitcher; Tommy Henrich, outfielder; Joe DiMaggio, outfielder; Allie Reynolds, pitcher; and Yogi Berra, catcher.*

Right: *The Dodgers' Duke Snider is forced at second by the Braves in 1949. Eddie Stanky threw to Alvin Dark, whose relay trying to double up Jackie Robinson was wild.*

ending double play. Though a notable power hitter who rarely bunted, Henrich asked manager Joe McCarthy for permission to lay one down. McCarthy consented. Henrich bunted to keep the inning alive, and DiMaggio doubled. Unquestionably the people's choice, Joltin' Joe won the Most Valuable Player Award. "DiMaggio's. . .stance toward life – a steely will, understated style, relentless consistency – was mesmerizing to a nation that knew it would soon need what he epitomized, heroism for the long haul," wrote George F. Will.

Incredibly, the Series was almost as entertaining as the season – most notably, when Dodger catcher Mickey Owen dropped a would-be game-ending strike three in pivotal Game Four. The Yankees rallied to win and take an insurmountable 3-1 lead in games. There followed the celebrated joke of wartime baseball. Except that it wasn't so laughable at all. In 1942 all but 71 big leaguers were in baseball uniforms, and the season's high standards proved it. In 1943-45 many all-stars were overseas, but the players left behind conducted themselves admirably. Sure, the era was known for 1944, the season the St. Louis Browns won their only pennant while 15-year-old Joe Nuxhall pitched for the Reds, and 1945, the year of one-armed outfielder Pete Gray and wooden-legged hurler Bert Shepard. Let's keep our eyes on the ball: the Browns were legitimate champions. Gray, who batted .218, and Nuxhall and Shepard, who pitched one game apiece in '44 and '45, respectively, were anomalies.

In "A Fresh Look at Wartime Baseball," a paper he presented to the 1991 convention of the Society for American Baseball Research (SABR), David M. Jordan argued convincingly on behalf of the 1942-45 seasons. "While many of the big stars were gone – superstars like Williams, Feller, DiMaggio and Greenberg – there were still superstars who remained – like Musial and Ott – and quite a few others nearly in that category such as Boudreau, Doerr, Medwick and Wynn. Many of the other players who went off to the service were just average players, and the men who replaced *them* were often only marginally inferior, if at all, to those for whom they were filling in. Since there were only 400 big-league jobs then, there were many more high-quality players in the minor leagues than there are now. When these players filled the big-league rosters during the war, quality of play only marginally diminished."

You'd have expected the star pitchers who played wartime ball to have feasted on inferior opponents and lapsed in peacetime. Not so, says Jordan. Hal Newhouser, twice an MVP during the war, continued his fine pace when the veterans returned. As for wartime hitters, their war-year stats were not much better – if at all – than their lifetime averages.

But it's unquestionably true that postwar baseball was better than ever. In 1946 the Cardinals beat the Dodgers in the first pennant playoff since 1908, then edged the Red Sox in a wonderful seven-game Series. The following season baseball decided that America, having fought the world's worst bigots overseas, was ready to inaugurate a non-racist national pastime at home. In the game's most notable sociological development, Brooklyn's Jackie Robinson in 1947 became major-league baseball's first black player and, arguably, the first significant postwar achievement of the civil rights movement. The Dodgers lost the World Series to the Yanks, but not before Cookie Lavagetto broke up Bill Bevens's no-hitter, and left fielder Al Gionfriddo robbed Joe DiMaggio in one of the game's most celebrated catches. Fittingly, 1947 was the first year NBC began televising ballgames.

What could baseball possibly do for an encore? In 1948 the Indians beat the Red Sox in the American League's first pennant playoff. The next year Casey Stengel was signed to manage the Yankees, and the Yankees and Red Sox went to the final weekend of a pennant race so classic even David Halberstam consented to chronicle it. The Yankees needed wins in both games. They got the first, then the second when a little-noted batsman named Jerry Coleman sliced an excuse-me three-run double down the right-field line.

Floyd Giebell and Jimmy Wilson would have understood perfectly.

THE STREAK
Joe DiMaggio's 56-Game Hitting Streak

Opposite: *The Yanks' Joe DiMaggio scores on a Bill Dickey single during the '41 season, sliding needlessly while teammates watch from the dugout.*

Above: *Wrapped against the April 14, 1941 cold, DiMaggio signs autographs before the season opener in Yankee Stadium. By midseason his record 56-game hitting streak was being followed all over the country. In one dusty Montana cafe, ranchhands and farmhands reported for breakfast. As each saw a newspaper on the counter, he asked the proprietor, "He get one yesterday?" No one had to ask, "Who's he?"*

Left: *DiMaggio awaits his turn at bat on July 18, when he finally ran out of hits before 67,468 fans in Cleveland.*

Pages 112-13: *During his record streak, DiMaggio showed his classic follow-through before a crowd in Washington D.C. on June 26.*

.406
Ted Williams Cracks a Barrier in 1941

Left: *American League manager Del Baker gives Ted Williams a kiss for winning the 1941 All-Star Game 7-5 with a two-on, two-out, ninth-inning homer. The Kid hit like this all year en route to baseball's last .400 season.*

Below: *The Yankees' Charlie "King Kong" Keller and Williams gird for a September shootout in Fenway Park. Williams edged Keller 37-33 for the home run title, but DiMaggio beat Williams in RBIs 125-120 and was named MVP in close balloting.*

Opposite: *There was nothing frivolous about The Thumper's approach to hitting. In '41 he returned to the lineup after only two weeks off with a broken ankle and kept it taped all year. In deference to the ankle he did cut down on his swing – possibly to the benefit of his batting average.*

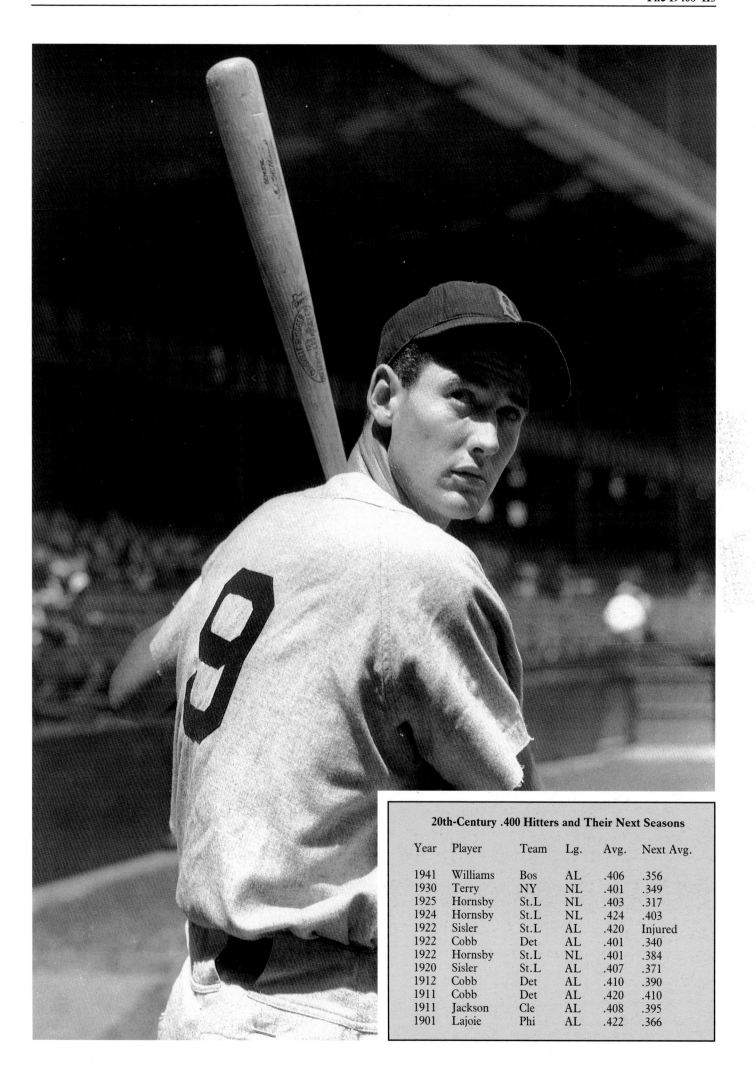

20th-Century .400 Hitters and Their Next Seasons

Year	Player	Team	Lg.	Avg.	Next Avg.
1941	Williams	Bos	AL	.406	.356
1930	Terry	NY	NL	.401	.349
1925	Hornsby	St.L	NL	.403	.317
1924	Hornsby	St.L	NL	.424	.403
1922	Sisler	St.L	AL	.420	Injured
1922	Cobb	Det	AL	.401	.340
1922	Hornsby	St.L	NL	.401	.384
1920	Sisler	St.L	AL	.407	.371
1912	Cobb	Det	AL	.410	.390
1911	Cobb	Det	AL	.420	.410
1911	Jackson	Cle	AL	.408	.395
1901	Lajoie	Phi	AL	.422	.366

Opposite: *Williams hit using a classic uppercut swing.*

Right: *Greeted by DiMaggio (left) and Detroit coach Marvin Shea, Williams crosses the plate after homering off the Cubs' Claude Passeau to win the 1941 All-Star game. "Williams, laughing, clapping his hands, leaping like a young colt, bounded his way around the base paths and touched home plate,"* Robert W. Creamer *wrote in* Baseball in '41. *"The All Stars on the American League bench ran toward home plate to pound Williams on the back . . . . There had been dramatic moments in earlier All Star games . . . . But Williams' homer . . . made this the first truly exciting All Star game, and in half a century since there hasn't been another to top it."*

Below: *Protecting his .410 average on August 11 "the way the RAF protects the British coast," according to a UPI cutline, Williams triples in Fenway Park.*

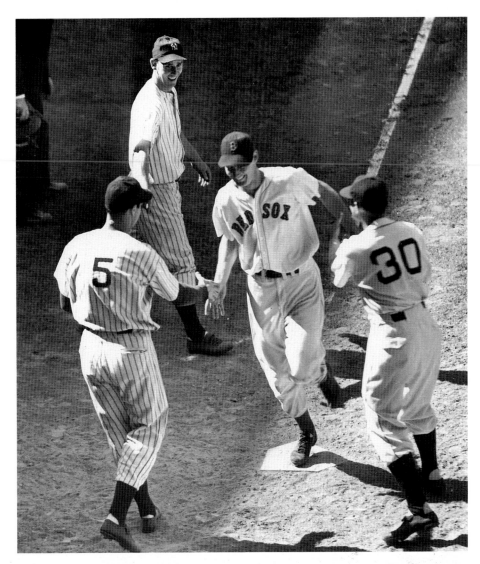

ONE THAT GOT AWAY
The 1941 World Series

Left: *At 37, crafty Yankee veteran Red Ruffing beat the Dodgers 3-2 in the opening game of the 1941 Series.*

Opposite top: *A man and a moment to remember. After the Yankees' Tommy Henrich swung and missed the strike three that should have ended Game Four, Dodger catcher Mickey Owen allowed the pitch to get by him, enabling Henrich to reach first. The Yankees rallied from a 4-3 deficit to win 7-4 and took the Series finale the next day. For his part Owen became an all-time Series goat, although some think the fatal pitch (thrown by Hugh Casey) had been a hard-to-catch spitter. The Dodgers still had the lead with two outs and just one baserunner, so the passed ball shouldn't have been fatal. Yet the easily-rattled Casey quickly lost his stuff, and manager Leo Durocher unaccountably left him in to absorb a pounding.*

Opposite bottom: *Dodger pitcher Whit Wyatt and manager Leo Durocher (2) protest a walk in Game Five. The Yankees won 3-1 to wrap up the Series.*

36-Year-Old Starting World Series Pitchers (1919-1969)

Player	Team	Series	Age	Record
Walter Johnson	Senators	1924	36	1-2
Stanley Coveleski	Senators	1925	36	0-2
Walter Johnson	Senators	1925	37	2-1
Grover Alexander	Cardinals	1926	39	2-0
Urban Shocker	Yankees	1926	36	0-1
Grover Alexander	Cardinals	1928	41	0-1
Jack Quinn	Athletics	1929	45	0-0
Burleigh Grimes	Cardinals	1930	36	0-2
Jesse Haines	Cardinals	1930	36	1-0
Burleigh Grimes	Cardinals	1931	37	2-0
Charlie Root	Cubs	1935	36	0-1
General Crowder	Tigers	1935	36	1-0
Jim Turner	Reds	1940	36	0-1
Red Ruffing	Yankees	1941	37	1-0
Curt Davis	Dodgers	1941	37	0-1
Fred Fitzsimmons	Dodgers	1941	39	0-0
Red Ruffing	Yankees	1942	38	1-1
Claude Passeau	Cubs	1945	36	1-0
Ray Prim	Cubs	1945	38	0-1
Bobo Newsom	Yankees	1947	39	0-1
Nelson Potter	Braves	1948	36	0-0
Allie Reynolds	Yankees	1951	36	1-1
Allie Reynolds	Yankees	1952	37	2-1
Preacher Roe	Dodgers	1952	37	1-0
Allie Reynolds	Yankees	1953	38	1-0
Preacher Roe	Dodgers	1953	38	0-1
Sal Maglie	Giants	1954	37	0-0
Sal Maglie	Dodgers	1956	39	1-1
Warren Spahn	Braves	1957	36	1-1
Warren Spahn	Braves	1958	37	2-1
Early Wynn	White Sox	1959	39	1-1

BASEBALL GOES TO WAR

Opposite: *Detroit slugger Hank Greenberg (center) and a smiling group of messmates at Fort Custer, Michigan. One of the first players drafted in World War II, Greenberg, then 31, was inducted into the Army only 19 games through the 1941 season. He didn't return to the Tigers until midway through the 1945 season. No worse from the layoff, he hit a ninth-inning homer on the final day of the season to win the pennant.*

Above: *Ted Williams is sworn in as a naval aviation cadet in May 1942. He flew missions in both World War II and Korea.*

Right: *Joe DiMaggio giving an autograph to Captain Raymond Spuhler of Johnstown, Pennsylvania while on tour of the Far East in 1950.*

Page 122: *Posing beside his guns on a cold winter day in 1943, Bob (then called Bobby) Feller was the Navy captain of a 40 mm. gun crew.*

Page 123: *Three former big leaguers rendezvous at a camp in the Pacific. From left: Big Jim Bivin (Pirates and Phillies), Long Tom Winsett (Red Sox), and Calvin "Preacher" Dorsett (Indians).*

THE BROWNIES' MOMENT OF GREATNESS FLICKERS

The Browns Were the Last Team to Win Their First Pennant		
Franchise	League	1st Pennant
Boston	NL	1877
Brooklyn	NL	1890
Chicago	NL	1876
Cincinnati	NL	1919
New York	NL	1888
Pittsburgh	NL	1901
Philadelphia	NL	1915
St. Louis	NL	1926
Boston	AL	1903
Chicago	AL	1901
Cleveland	AL	1920
Detroit	AL	1907
New York	AL	1921
Philadelphia	AL	1902
St. Louis	AL	1944
Washington	AL	1924

Opposite top: *More than 33,000 fans jammed St. Louis's Sportsman's Park for the 1944 World Series between two crosstown rivals, the Cardinals and Browns. Here the Browns' second baseman Don Gutteridge leads off the opener. The Browns won 2-1 behind Denny Galehouse.*

Opposite bottom: *An aerial view of Sportsman's Park, where all six games of the Series were played. The Cardinals took the exciting Series four games to two.*

Above: *The Browns' George McQuinn is greeted at the plate after his two-run homer in the Series opener gave his team the winning margin over the Cards.*

Right: *Cardinal pitcher Max Lanier was safe when Brown pitcher Nelson Potter bobbled his bunt and threw wildly for two errors in the second game. The Cardinals won 3-2 in 11 innings, and went on to take the Series four games to two.*

THE 4F LEAGUE

Left: *Pete Gray, a one-armed leftfielder, batted .218 over 77 games for the Browns in 1945, his only big-league season.*

Opposite top: *Reunited after the war, the 1946 Cardinals head for another World Series. From left: Joe Garagiola, Dick Sisler, George "Whitey" Kurowski, Enos Slaughter and Stan Musial.*

Opposite bottom: *The Reds' manager Bill McKechnie and 15-year-old Joe Nuxhall, who became the youngest player in major league history when he hurled in one game during the 1944 season. Predictably butchered by opposing hitters, he was sentenced to the minors with a 45.00 ERA.*

Representative Wartime and Lifetime Batting Records			
Player	Wartime Seasons	Wartime BA	Lifetime BA
Luke Appling	three	.299	.310
Lou Boudreau	four	.301	.295
Phil Cavarretta	four	.309	.293
Bobby Doerr	three	.293	.288
Bob Elliott	four	.300	.289
Stan Hack	four	.301	.301
Tommy Holmes	four	.303	.302
Bob Johnson	four	.291	.296
George Kell	two	.270	.306
Charlie Keller	three	.284	.286
Joe Kuhel	four	.257	.277
Whitey Kurowski	four	.286	.286
Ernie Lombardi	four	.297	.306
Marty Marion	four	.275	.263
Frank McCormick	four	.289	.299
George McQuinn	four	.258	.276
Joe Medwick	four	.302	.324
Wally Moses	four	.272	.291
Stan Musial	three	.341	.331
Mel Ott	four	.284	.304
Elmer Valo	two	.240	.282
Arky Vaughan	two	.292	.318
Dixie Walker	four	.313	.306
Gee Walker	four	.252	.294
George Case	four	.290	.282
Tony Cuccinello	four	.273	.280
Jeff Heath	four	.289	.293
Snuffy Stirnweiss	three	.297	.268

RED SOX HEARTACHES

Upper left: *Yankee shortstop Johnny Lindell is forced at second on a throw from Boston second baseman Bobby Doerr (left) to Johnny Pesky, whose relay to first doubled up Nick Etten to end the first game of a doubleheader in August 1946. When Pesky delayed throwing home in the '46 World Series, Enos Slaughter scored the winning run. Pesky's designation as Series goat seems unfair, however, because Slaughter had an excellent jump.*

Left: *Ted Williams with the DiMaggio brothers Joe (left) and Dominick. Stifled by the "Boudreau shift" that placed three and sometimes four fielders between first and second, Williams was held to five singles in the '46 Series.*

Opposite top: *New Boston manager Joe McCarthy, late of the Yankees, talks to Red Sox before the 1948 season. In another heartbreaker, they lost the pennant to Cleveland in a one-game playoff.*

Opposite bottom: *Enos Slaughter scores the winning run against Boston in the 1946 Series.*

CUBS WIN!
The Chicago Cubs of 1945

Chicago Cub Pennant Winners

Year	Record	Manager	World Series
1906	116-36	Frank Chance	Lost 4-2
1907	107-45	Frank Chance	Won 4-0-1
1908	99-55	Frank Chance	Won 4-1
1910	104-50	Frank Chance	Lost 4-1
1918	84-45	Fred Mitchell	Lost 4-2
1929	98-54	Joe McCarthy	Lost 4-1
1932	90-64	Hornsby/Grimm	Lost 4-0
1935	100-54	Charlie Grimm	Lost 4-3
1938	89-63	Grimm/Hartnett	Lost 4-0
1945	98-56	Charlie Grimm	Lost 4-3

Opposite: *Cub manager Charlie Grimm barks orders. Grimm skippered the Cubs to a pennant in 1945, with a 98-56 record. His fragmented managing career in Chicago encompassed 1932-1938, 1944-1949, and 1960.*

Above: *The Cubs' classy centerfielder, Andy Pafko, harnessed the 1945 pennant express with 110 RBIs.*

Upper right: *Versatile Paul Derringer won 16 games and led the Cubs with four saves in 1945.*

Lower right: *Redoubtable Phil Cavarretta won the '45 National League batting title with a .355 average, and led both teams (.423) in the Series.*

Pages 132-33: *Cavarretta was safe at the plate on Pafko's fourth-inning triple in Game Seven of the '45 Series, when Detroit catcher Paul Richards dropped the ball. Nonetheless, the Tigers took the finale 9-3.*

THE MEXICAN CHALLENGE – A NEW LEAGUE

Above left: *Red Steiner, an AL catcher in 1945, joined Mexico's La Junta team for the '46 season.*

Above: *Former Dodger Luis Olmo played in a Mexican minor league.*

Left: *Bernardo Pasquel (left), owner of the Mexican League, arrives in Mexico City with his newest signee, former Cardinal shortstop Lou Klein. The wealthy Pasquel brothers lured players by offering higher salaries. The Mexican League never really got off the ground, with the first of the jumpers – Mickey Owen – returning to the States in August.*

Opposite top left: *Danny Gardella, a onetime Giant outfielder, played with Vera Cruz. When the majors blacklisted him, he sued in federal court, threatening the reserve clause, and got an off-the-docket settlement.*

Opposite top right: *Former minor leaguer Ray Brown joined Laguna.*

Opposite bottom: *Fans fill the stands for a game in Mexico City.*

JACKIE RESTORES BASEBALL'S SOUL
Baseball Integrates in 1947

First Blacks in the Majors after World War II

Date	Player	Team
4-15-1947	*Jackie Robinson	Brooklyn Dodgers
7-4-1947	Larry Doby	Cleveland Indians
7-17-1947	Henry Thompson	St. Louis Browns
7-19-1947	Willard Brown	St. Louis Browns
8-26-1947	Dan Bankhead	Brooklyn Dodgers
4-20-1948	*Roy Campanella	Brooklyn Dodgers
7-8-1948	*Satchel Paige	Cleveland Indians
4-19-1949	Minnie Minoso	Cleveland Indians
5-20-1949	Don Newcombe	Brooklyn Dodgers
7-8-1949	*Monte Irvin	New York Giants
8-11-1949	Luke Easter	Cleveland Indians
4-18-1950	Sam Jethroe	Boston Braves

Hall of Fame member

Opposite: *In Havana, Cuba for spring training with the Montreal Royals – the Dodgers' top farm club – Jackie Robinson studies the Dodger roster in March of 1947. He would soon be added to it as the first black major leaguer of the 20th century.*

Above: *Dodger president Branch Rickey and three of his stars at Yankee Stadium await the 1949 World Series. From left: Gil Hodges, Gene Hermanski, Jackie Robinson.*

Right: *In his first appearance with the Dodgers during an exhibition game against the Yankees in April 1947, first baseman Robinson reaches for a high throw while the Yanks' Phil Rizzuto reaches base.*

Above: *By June of 1951 Robinson was a central character on a more integrated team. From left: Duke Snider, Hodges, Robinson, Pee Wee Reese, Roy Campanella.*

Left: *Don Newcombe (center) is greeted by Robinson and Campanella when he joins the Dodgers in 1949. Big Newk went 17-8 as a rookie.*

Opposite: *Satchel Paige is shown pitching for Grover Cleveland Alexander while a member of the New York Black Yankees in 1941. Seven years later he helped the Cleveland Indians win a pennant.*

CASEY TAKES THE SPOTLIGHT
Casey Stengel Becomes Yankee Manager in '49

Opposite: *"I see a bright future,"*
Casey Stengel said upon being hired
to manage the Yankees in 1949. He
was right: He won 10 pennants and
seven world championships in 12
years.

Right: *Casey gives his troops a pep*
talk. "The secret of managing," he
once said, "is to keep the five guys
who hate you from the five guys who
are undecided."

Below: *Stengel arguing with an*
umpire during a game against the
Tigers. The next day they were
undoubtedly old friends again. "I
can't hold a hate," said the Old
Professor.

Below right: *In 1950 Stengel*
conferred with former Yankee
manager Joe McCarthy (left) during
pre-game festivities at Yankee
Stadium honoring the 50th
anniversary of the American League.
Stengel himself became an ex-Yankee
manager 10 years later, when the
Yankees dumped him purportedly as
part of a youth movement. "I'll never
make the mistake of being 70 again,"
he said.

BUMS NO MORE
The 1947 Brooklyn Dodgers

Opposite top: *The Dodgers parade through Brooklyn after clinching the 1947 National League pennant.*

Opposite bottom: *Cookie Lavagetto's ninth-inning double not only broke up Bill Bevens's no-hitter but broke Yankee hearts. Thanks to Cookie's timely shot, the Dodgers won Game Four of the '47 Series 2-1.*

Above: *Fred "Dixie" Walker. Known as "The People's Cherce," the Georgian drove in 94 runs and hit .306 for the '47 Dodgers.*

Above right: *Shortstop Pee Wee Reese got his nickname from shooting marbles, not for being 5' 10". Few Dodgers ever loomed larger in the middle infield.*

Right: *Burt Shotton, new Dodger manager in 1947, is congratulated by Giant counterpart Mel Ott. Shotton won flags in '47 and '49.*

SPAHN AND SAIN AND PRAY FOR RAIN
The 1948 Braves

Opposite top: *The Boston Braves' Warren Spahn shows his Hall of Fame pitching style as he warms up for a game in September 1948.*

Opposite bottom: *The Braves' shortstop Alvin Dark (here relaying to first for a double play) hit .322 as a mainstay on Boston's '48 pennant winners – their first since 1914.*

Above: *Southpaw Warren Spahn (left) and righthanded Johnny Sain were basically a two-man pitching staff for the '48 Braves. While Spahn went 15-12, logging 257 innings, and Sain led the National League with 24 wins, 28 complete games and 315 innings, the Braves' fans chanted "Spahn and Sain and pray for rain." Unfortunately, there wasn't enough rain in the World Series, and the Braves fell to the Indians in six.*

Right: *One of five .300 hitters in the Braves' lineup, Tommy Holmes batted .325, with 35 doubles and only 20 strikeouts in 1948.*

THE GREAT STAN "THE MAN" MUSIAL

Opposite: *A sequential shot of Stan Musial's batting style. Arguably the greatest Cardinal and one of the most dominant players of the 1940s, Musial was called "The Man" because fearful fans at Ebbets Field would say, "Here comes the man."*

Above: *Before a game with the Dodgers, Musial looks over some pictures of himself and other players presented to him by twins promoting a well-known dessert of the time.*

Right: *Musial is honored in 1963 during his last visit to Los Angeles. In St. Louis there's a statue of him outside Busch Stadium.*

THE YANKEES TAKE WING – 1949

Opposite top: *Yankee manager Casey Stengel hands the ball to his ace reliever Joe Page, who saved a league-leading 27 games in 1949.*

Opposite bottom: *Tommy Henrich scores after homering for the only run in the '49 Series opener against Brooklyn. The Yankees won the first of five consecutive world titles.*

Right: *Allie Reynolds joined the Yankees in 1947 and led the league in winning percentage. Between 1947 and 1953, Superchief went 7-2 in World Series competition, with two wins and four saves as a reliever.*

Below: *On the last day of the '49 season Jerry Coleman clinched the pennant with a bases-loaded double.*

BASEBALL TRANSFORMED
Baseball's Modern Look After War

Opposite top: *After four years in the service, Detroit's Hank Greenberg was back in hitting form. Here he awaits the pitch from A's Bobo Newsom.*

Opposite bottom: *Postwar attendance at ballparks boomed. Some 35,000 fans jam Fenway Park to witness the 1946 All-Star game after a one-year wartime interruption.*

Above: *Baseball's labor relations were just as one-sided in management's favor after World War II as they had been before. Bob Murphy of the American Baseball Guild knocks in vain on the Pirates' clubhouse door before a Pirates-Giants game in June 1946. Inside the players voted down a strike. Murphy did negotiate per diem expenses, still called "Murphy money."*

Right: *Commissioner Happy Chandler throws out the first ball at the 1950 World Series. Chandler's tenure as Commissioner would end the following year, when he angered club owners by trying to monitor their activities in premature signings of high school players.*

High and Low Franchise Attendance during the 1940s							
Franchise	League	Year	High	Finish	Year	Low	Finish
Boston	NL	1948	1,455,439	1st	1944	208,691	6th
Brooklyn	NL	1947	1,807,526	1st	1944	605,905	7th
Chicago	NL	1947	1,364,039	6th	1943	508,247	5th
Cincinnati	NL	1947	899,975	5th	1945	290,070	7th
New York	NL	1947	1,600,793	4th	1943	466,095	8th
Philadelphia	NL	1946	1,045,247	5th	1940	207,177	8th
Pittsburgh	NL	1948	1,517,021	4th	1942	448,897	5th
St. Louis	NL	1949	1,430,676	2nd	1944	461,968	1st
Boston	AL	1949	1,596,650	2nd	1943	358,275	7th
Chicago	AL	1946	983,403	5th	1942	425,734	6th
Cleveland	AL	1948	2,620,627	1st	1943	438,894	3rd
Detroit	AL	1949	1,821,204	4th	1943	606,287	5th
New York	AL	1948	2,373,901	3rd	1943	645,006	1st
Philadelphia	AL	1948	945,076	4th	1943	376,735	8th
St. Louis	AL	1944	508,644	1st	1941	176,240	6th
Washington	AL	1946	1,027,216	4th	1940	381,241	7th

DECADE HIGHLIGHTS

Decade Leaders, 1940-49

	National League		American League	
Batting				
BA	Stan Musial	.346	Ted Williams	.356
HRs	John Mize	217	Ted Williams	234
RBIs	Bob Elliott	903	Ted Williams	893
Hits	Bob Elliott	1563	Lou Boudreau	1578
Runs	Stan Musial	815	Ted Williams	951
2B	Stan Musial	302	Lou Boudreau	339
SB	Pee Wee Reese	108	George Case	285
BB	Bob Elliott	728	Ted Williams	992
Pitching				
Wins	Mort Cooper	114	Hal Newhouser	190
ERA	Harry Brecheen	2.71	Hal Newhouser	2.83
SO	Mort Cooper	772	Hal Newhouser	1579
IP	Mort Cooper	1606	Hal Newhouser	2458

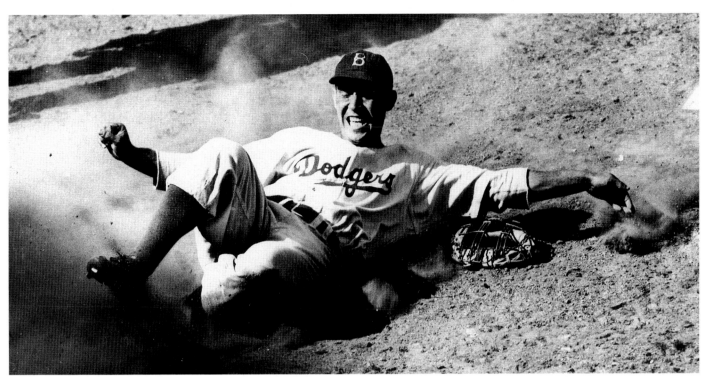

Opposite: *Cleveland shortstop-manager Lou Boudreau is thrown out trying to stretch a double in the 1948 World Series, but he did lead the Fall Classic with four two-baggers and 14 assists. All of which followed an MVP (.355, 106 RBIs, 116 runs, .534 slugging percentage) season that ended with two homers in the playoff victory over Boston.*

Above: *At 21 Dodger outfielder Pete Reiser (here stealing home) was the 1941 National League leader in batting (.343), doubles (39), triples (17), runs (117), and slugging (.558). Because of collisions with unpadded outfield walls, however, he had only four 100-game seasons.*

Right: *Only Babe Ruth homered more frequently than Pirate great Ralph Kiner, who led the National League seven straight times, had 369 taters in 10 years and hit one every 14 at bats.*

Pages 154-55: *Joe "Flash" Gordon, scoring on a close play at home, played in five World Series as a Yank and Indian second baseman in the 1940s.*

407 FT.

It has become fashionable of late to deride baseball in the 1950s. "The baseball of the 1950s was perhaps the most one-dimensional, uniform, predictable version of the game that has ever been offered for sale," contends *The Bill James Historical Baseball Abstract*. "By 1950, the stolen base was a rare play, a 'surprise' play."

The critics drone on. Teams would get a man on base and wait for some Baby Huey type – a Rocky Colavito, Jim Lemon or Gus Zernial – to drive them home. The average length of a game rose 15 minutes. Attendance declined – a development almost universally blamed on television but owed equally to people moving away from deteriorating central-city stadiums. Finally – this is the cry of a thousand American existentialists – the Dodgers left Brooklyn and destroyed our innocence forever.

Happily, there's a stronger case on behalf of the fifties. Baseball expanded its player pool by integrating – fifties baseball was eight percent black, according to James – but without adding teams. It was the only full decade in which the best players available were competing for only 400 roster spots. Talk about talent-intensive: fifties baseball was second to none.

There were more joys. O.K., we wish the Dodgers hadn't left for L.A., but baseball had legitimate new markets. The Giants moved from New York to San Francisco, the Braves from Boston to Milwaukee, the Browns from St. Louis to Baltimore (where they were renamed the Orioles), and the Athletics from Philadelphia to Kansas City. Suddenly, we had ourselves a bona fide *national* pastime.

But the proof is in the playing. Arguably baseball's three most ballyhooed single-game pitching, hitting and fielding feats occurred during the decade: Don Larsen's perfect game in the 1956 Series, Bobby Thomson's "Shot Heard 'round the World" in the 1951 pennant playoff, and Willie Mays's spectacular catch in the 1954 Series.

In *The 10 Best Years of Baseball: An Informal History of the Fifties*, Harold Rosenthal cited a 1976 poll to determine baseball's 10 most memorable baseball personalities. The results, in order of popularity: Babe Ruth,

Casey Stengel, Dizzy Dean, Willie Mays, Ted Williams, Mickey Mantle and Hank Aaron (tie), Roberto Clemente, Ty Cobb, and Jackie Robinson. Take note: Seven of the 10 – everyone but Cobb, Dean and Ruth – were active in the fifties. You could argue that Mays was baseball's greatest all-around everyday player, Williams its greatest hitter, Aaron its greatest slugger and Robinson its greatest hero.

For pure theater, no decade eclipsed the fifties. It was more than New York press agentry that the three greatest centerfielders of the decade played for the New York teams in Manhattan, the Bronx and Brooklyn. Was your favorite Willie (Mays), Mickey (Mantle) or the Duke (Duke Snider)? Of such things are great songs written. The Giants' comeback in 1951 was possibly the most stirring ever, and their upset victory over the powerful (111-43) Indians in the '54 Series was one of the most unexpected. Not even the fifties baseball movie, *Damn Yankees*, stirred the heartstrings more than the Dodgers' first world championship a year later – unless you count the 1959 game in which Harvey Haddix, a 33-year-old Pittsburgh southpaw, pitched a 12-inning perfect game, only to lose in the 13th. Other tear-jerking favorites: Milwaukee's world title in 1957, the first of the modern era by a relocated franchise; Mickey Mantle's Triple Crown in 1956; and 39-year-old Ted Williams's .388 average in 1957. The decade ended on an especially pleasing note, when the "go-go" Chicago White Sox resurrected the running game.

How do we explain fifties winners? Certainly integration had much to do with results. Among the National League's pennant winners, only the 1950 Phillies were all-white. The 1954 Cleveland Indians and 1959 Chicago White Sox won flags with significant contributions from blacks and Hispanics.

But the decade belonged to the Yankees, who didn't integrate until 1955 and whose personnel was only marginally superior to that of other contenders. To explain New York's eight pennants and six world championships, we must turn to the baseball figure of the decade.

Pages 156-57: *Don Larsen throws the first pitch of his perfect game – call it Grand Larceny – in the 1956 World Series.*

Left: *Ted Williams was going strong in his third decade as a home run hitter.*

Opposite top: *Dodgers embrace Johnny Podres after he beat the Yankees 2-0 in the 1955 Series finale for Brooklyn's only world championship.*

Opposite bottom: *Bobby Thomson (left) celebrates his 1951 pennant-winning homer with teammates Larry Jansen and Sal Maglie.*

It wasn't Mickey Mantle, Whitey Ford or Yogi Berra. Mr. 1950s was Casey Stengel.

The first modern manager, Casey simply got more out of his men than did his peers. If a player was too weak or inexperienced to play full time, Stengel platooned him (a practice he retained from the 1920s, when Casey himself had been platooned by John McGraw). The Old Professor used pinch hitters at will – even in the first inning. "I like good pinch hitters," he said. "I believe that with a lively ball that you've got to be an attacker. If I've got a good pinch hitter, I hate to see him stay on the bench with men on the bases in an early inning. He may end the game right there." Later in the game Stengel waved in slews of defensive replacements and relievers. Stengel had plenty of both, because he taught players to handle more than one position and made the bullpen closer to a noble calling. "We're paying 25 men, we might as well let them earn their money," he said.

In a sense, Casey was the antithesis of the age. Most managers feared they would be second-guessed for starting rookies or signing supposedly over-the-hill veterans. Casey had three Rookies-of-the-Year and two runners-up in the fifties, and he prolonged the careers of useful oldsters like Johnny Mize, Enos Slaughter and Jim Konstanty. Stengel's fellow skippers often thought of themselves as drill sergeants; Casey knew every player had to be treated differently. While other managers were waiting for the long ball, Stengel was teaching his players to go from first to third and perfect their bunting. Most AL skippers took fielding for granted. Casey had his outfielders throw six feet to the left of his relay men, because most infielders are righthanded, ya see, and they'd be lined up to throw home if they ran left to catch the ball. Funny thing: Other successful fifties managers like Al Lopez (who once caught for Casey) were equally innovative and aggressive.

So the "uniform, predictable" fifties were downright fascinating. You could look it up.

WHIZ KIDS – THE 1950 PHILLIES

Opposite: *Philly workhorse Robin Roberts went 20-11 in 1950 and led the league with five shutouts and 39 starts. He pitched almost as well in the Series, losing Game Two 2-1 in 10 innings.*

Right: *Second baseman Jimmy Bloodworth makes a great stop but loses the ball, allowing the Yanks' Phil Rizzuto to reach base in the ninth inning of the 1950 Series' third game. The Yankees went on to win it 3-2 when the next batter, Jerry Coleman, singled in the winning run.*

Below: *Rightfielder Del Ennis had a league-leading 126 RBIs to go with his .311 average for the Whiz Kids.*

Below right: *In 1950 batmeister Richie Ashburn, a lifetime .300 hitter, routinely hit .303, with an NL-best 14 triples. More surprisingly, centerfielder Ashburn, known for fleet feet and a somewhat anemic arm, gunned down the Dodgers' Cal Abrams at home to preserve a tie on the last day of the 1950 season. The Yanks swept the Whiz Kids in the Series, but the games were close.*

THE MIRACLE OF COOGAN'S BLUFF
The Giants' Pennant in 1951

Opposite: *Was any pitcher ever more accurately nicknamed than the Giants' Sal "The Barber" Maglie, who pitched 'em close as a razor and always looked as if he hadn't shaved in three days? Maglie was blade-sharp in 1951, when he went 23-6.*

Right: *How easily we forget that the Giants won a best-of-three playoff for the '51 pennant. Heroes of the 3-1 win in Game One: Thomson, who homered off Ralph Branca (this is no typo); pitcher Jim Hearn, the winner; and leftfielder Monte Irvin, who scored twice and homered for the insurance run.*

Below right: *Irvin had seven hits in the first two games of the '51 Series. Despite his Series-leading 11 hits, two stolen bases and .458 average, the Yankees won in six games.*

Below: *Giant manager Leo Durocher (left) hugs Bobby Thomson after his pennant-winning homer in 1951.*

Pages 164-65: *It's celebration time when Thomson rounds third after homering again off Branca with his "shot heard 'round the world" in decisive Game Three (Durocher is going crazy), scores (teammates await him) and heads for the clubhouse (it's every man for himself).*

WHO'S THE BEST?
Great New York Centerfielders of the Fifties

Center Fielder Decade Batting Stats													
Player	G	AB	R	H	RBI	2B	3B	HR	BA	OBA	SA	SB	BB
Mantle	1246	4478	994	1392	841	208	54	280	.311	.425	.569	98	893
Mays	1065	4074	777	1291	709	204	79	250	.315	.392	.590	179	504
Snider	1418	5219	970	1605	1031	274	57	326	.307	.390	.569	77	711
Ashburn	1523	5997	952	1875	422	252	82	19	.312	.396	.391	158	828
Doby	1236	4330	768	1225	816	194	40	215	.283	.385	.495	28	725

Opposite top: *At the Polo Grounds in August 1954 Willie Mays is honored with "Willie Mays Day," as thousands of fans cheer the 23-year-old sensation.*

Opposite bottom: *The prime centerfielders of the '50s – Mickey Mantle (left), Duke Snider and Willie Mays – together for the taping of a television sports program in later years. The trio compiled lofty career statistics and honors both at the plate and in the field.*

Right top: *Duke Snider gets a bat for each of the four homers he hit for Brooklyn in the 1952 World Series. Hoping for better things in '53, manager Chuck Dressen is ready to hand him a fifth.*

Right bottom: *Yankee Mickey Mantle is greeted by teammate Yogi Berra after homering in the 1956 All-Star game. The clout was a mere footnote in his Triple Crown year, when he batted .353 with 52 homers and 130 RBIs.*

Page 168 top: *As a 19-year-old rookie in 1951, Mantle faces Cleveland's immortal Bob Feller.*

Page 168 bottom: *Snider's magnificent catch robs Yogi Berra in Game Four of the 1952 Series. The Duke couldn't prevent Johnny Mize's previous shot from going out, and the Yankees won 2-0.*

Page 169: *Willie Mays demonstrates his swing in 1954, the year his MVP performance helped the Giants take the pennant and the world championship.*

YANKS ROLL. . .
1951

Yankee Pennant-Winners and the Second-Place Clubs During the 1950s			
	W	L	GB
1950 New York	98	56	–
Detroit	95	59	3
1951 New York	98	56	–
Cleveland	93	61	5
1952 New York	95	59	–
Cleveland	93	61	2
1953 New York	99	52	–
Cleveland	92	62	8.5
1955 New York	96	58	–
Cleveland	93	61	3
1956 New York	97	57	–
Cleveland	88	66	9
1957 New York	98	56	–
Chicago	90	64	8
1958 New York	92	62	–
Chicago	82	72	10

Opposite top: *Joe DiMaggio (left) breaks in his successor as Yankee centerfielder, Mickey Mantle, in 1951. They started together in the '51 Series, with DiMag in center and the Mick in right.*

Opposite bottom: *Yankee catcher Yogi Berra drops a foul pop by Ted Williams for what would have been the last out in Allie Reynolds's second no-hitter of the 1951 season. No matter: Williams popped up the next pitch, and Berra caught it.*

Right: *Vic Raschi averaged 18.5 wins a year for the 1948-53 Yankees. In 1951 his league-leading 164 strikeouts helped the Bombers win the pennant.*

Below: *Gene Woodling scores after homering. Platooned judiciously by manager Casey Stengel, the Yankee outfielder led the league with a .429 on-base percentage in 1953.*

. . .AND YANKS ROLL. . .
1952

Opposite top: *Eddie Lopat lost the third game of the 1952 Series 5-2, but the little lefty and three other Yankee pitchers masterminded a 4-2 win in decisive Game Seven.*

Opposite bottom: *Five of the six Yankees scheduled to play in the 1952 All-Star game await action with manager Casey Stengel. From left: Mickey Mantle, outfielder; Hank Bauer, outfielder; Stengel; Allie Reynolds, pitcher; Yogi Berra, catcher; Phil Rizzuto, shortstop. Pitcher Vic Raschi is not pictured.*

Above: *Allie Reynolds is surrounded by teammates after beating the Dodgers 2-0 in the fourth game of the '52 Series to tie it up at two apiece.*

Right: *Billy Martin's desperation catch of Jackie Robinson's high pop with the bases loaded in Game Seven saved the Series for the Yankees, who won the finale 4-2.*

. . .AND YANKS ROLL!
1953

Above: *Gil McDougald scores after slugging a two-run homer in Game Four of the 1953 Series. The Yankees lost 7-3 to the Dodgers, but won the Series four games to two.*

Left: *Mantle celebrates his grand slam in Game Five. The Yankees won 11-7.*

Opposite: *A whole host of stars accounted for the Yankees' 9-5 win in the Series opener. From left: Hank Bauer, who singled and tripled; Yogi Berra, who singled and homered; Billy Martin, who hit a three-run triple; and Joe Collins, who hit the go-ahead homer.*

WHAT A TEAM!
The 1954 Indians

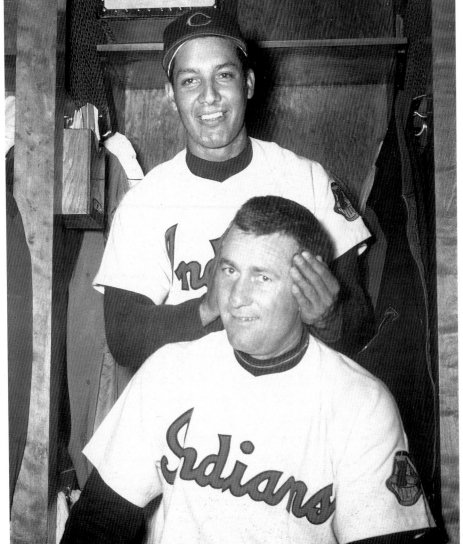

Above: *Manager Al Lopez (left) and his three star pitchers on the 1954 Cleveland Indians: Mike Garcia (19-8, league-leading 2.64 ERA), Bob Lemon (23-7) and Early Wynn (23-11). Behind a staff that posted an unreal 2.78 ERA – almost a full run below the league average – the Indians set an American League record of 111 wins, besting the second-place Yankees by eight games.*

Left: *Bob Lemon gets a "Dutch rub" from Indian outfielder and batting champion Bobby Avila (.341).*

Opposite: *Despite suffering a broken finger that permanently affected his grip and shortened his career, third baseman Al Rosen hit .300, with 24 homers and 102 RBIs. But what a run the 1953 MVP had: Between 1950 and 1954 he averaged .298, 31 homers and 114 RBIs.*

THE BIG UPSET
The 1954 World Series

Above left and right, and opposite top left: *In the eighth inning of the 1954 Series opener, the Giants' Willie Mays made his Catch Seen 'round the World when he robbed Cleveland's Vic Wertz of a hit that would have scored at least two runs. The Giants won 5-2 in 10 innings.*

Left: *New York's Johnny Antonelli, 21-7 during the '54 season, whipped the Indians 3-1 in Game Two.*

Opposite top right: *Series hero Dusty Rhodes won the opener with a homer, capped the next day's win with another four-bagger, then singled in two more scores during a 6-2 win in Game Three.*

Opposite bottom: *The great 1954 Indian pitching staff, bested by the Giants in a surprising Series sweep.*

Players Who Have Slugged 1.000 in World Series Play (5 or more ABs)						
Year	Player	Team	SlugAv	HR	R	RBI
1919	Dutch Ruether	Cin (NL)	1.500	0	2	4
1923	Babe Ruth	NY (AL)	1.000	3	8	3
1928	Lou Gehrig	NY (AL)	1.727	4	5	9
1928	Babe Ruth	NY (AL)	1.375	3	9	4
1932	Lou Gehrig	NY (AL)	1.118	3	9	8
1939	Charlie Keller	NY (AL)	1.188	3	8	6
1952	John Mize	NY (AL)	1.067	3	3	6
1954	Dusty Rhodes	NY (NL)	1.667	2	2	7
1961	John Blanchard	NY (AL)	1.100	2	4	3
1969	Donn Clendenon	NY (NL)	1.071	3	4	4

FINALLY, THE BUMS ARE THE BEST
The Dodgers' 1955 World Championship

Opposite top: *A circus catch in the sixth inning by Dodger leftfielder Sandy Amoros saved Game Seven and helped the 1955 Dodgers win their first world championship. After robbing Yankee Yogi Berra, Amoros threw to shortstop Pee Wee Reese, who relayed to first baseman Gil Hodges, doubling up Gil McDougald.*

Opposite bottom: *The Dodgers got heavy lumber indeed from Roy Campanella (left), Gil Hodges and Duke Snider, who had seven homers and 16 RBIs in the Series.*

Right: *Campy pinches the cheek of Johnny Podres, who had just beaten the Yankees 8-3 in the third game, aided by Campy's two-run homer.*

Below: *Jackie Robinson steals home in the opener.*

Pages 182-3: *Dodgers and fans rush joyously onto the field after the final out in Game Seven gives Brooklyn its long-awaited championship.*

MOVING DAY
Team Relocations of the Fifties

High and Low Franchise Attendance During the 1950s							
Franchise	League	Year	High	Finish	Year	Low	Finish
Boston	NL	1950	944,391	4th	1952	281,278	7th
Milwaukee		1957	2,215,404	1st	1953	1,826,397	2nd
Brooklyn	NL	1951	1,282,628	2nd	1954	1,020,531	2nd
Los Angeles		1959	2,071,045	1st	1958	1,845,556	7th
Chicago	NL	1950	1,165,944	7th	1957	670,629	7th
Cincinnati	NL	1956	1,125,928	3rd	1953	548,086	6th
New York	NL	1954	1,155,067	1st	1956	629,179	6th
San Francisco		1959	1,422,130	3rd	1958	1,272,625	3rd
Philadelphia	NL	1950	1,217,035	1st	1954	738,991	4th
Pittsburgh	NL	1959	1,359,917	4th	1955	469,397	8th
St. Louis	NL	1957	1,183,575	2nd	1955	849,130	7th
Boston	AL	1950	1,344,080	3rd	1954	931,127	4th
Chicago	AL	1959	1,423,144	1st	1950	781,330	6th
Cleveland	AL	1950	1,727,464	4th	1958	663,805	4th
Detroit	AL	1950	1,951,474	2nd	1953	884,658	6th
New York	AL	1950	2,081,380	1st	1958	1,428,438	1st
Philadelphia	AL	1952	627,100	4th	1954	304,666	8th
Kansas City		1955	1,393,054	6th	1957	901,067	7th
St. Louis	AL	1952	518,796	7th	1950	247,131	7th
Baltimore		1954	1,060,910	7th	1958	829,991	6th
Washington	AL	1950	699,697	5th	1955	425,238	8th

Above: *The last night game at New York's Polo Grounds, in 1957. The next season the Giants were playing in San Francisco.*

Opposite top left: *Vice-President Nixon throws out the first ball at Opening Day for the new Baltimore Orioles (formerly the St. Louis Browns), April 15, 1954.*

Opposite top right: *The 1958 Dodgers, Brooklyn Bums no more.*

Opposite bottom: *NL president Warren Giles awards the Braves' Hank Aaron a silver bat for his 1956 batting title. The Hall of Famer began his career with the Milwaukee Braves in 1954, a year after the franchise had moved from Boston.*

THE BRAVES WIN IT ALL IN '57

Opposite: *The Braves' Hank Aaron chases the Hank Bauer double that scored Jerry Coleman for the first run of the 1957 Series opener. The Yankees won 3-1.*

Right: *Milwaukee's Eddie Mathews could hit with the best of them (.292, 32 homers in '57), but his fine stop at third robbed Moose Skowron and provided the last out of the Series. "I'd made better plays," he said later, "but that big one in the spotlight stamped me the way I wanted to be remembered."*

Below: *Milwaukee's Bob Buhl throws the first pitch of Game Three to New York's Hank Bauer. Bauer bounced to Buhl, but the next batter, Tony Kubek, homered and the Yanks were off to a 12-3 romp.*

The Braves' Individual Statistics Leaders

Year	HRs		BA		Runs		RBIs		Wins		Strikeouts		ERA	
1953	Mathews	47	Mathews	.302	Mathews	110	Mathews	135	Spahn	23	Spahn	148	Spahn	2.10
1954	Mathews	40	Adcock	.308	Mathews	96	Mathews	103	Spahn	21	Spahn	136	Conley	2.96
1955	Mathews	41	Aaron	.314	Mathews	108	Aaron	106	Spahn	17	Buhl	117	Buhl	3.21
1956	Adcock	38	Aaron	.328	Aaron	106	Adcock	103	Spahn	20	Spahn	128	Burdette	2.70
1957	Aaron	44	Aaron	.322	Aaron	118	Aaron	132	Spahn	21	Buhl	117	Spahn	2.69
1958	Mathews	31	Aaron	.326	Aaron	109	Aaron	95	Spahn	22	Spahn	150	Burdette	2.91
1959	Mathews	46	Aaron	.355	Mathews	118	Aaron	123	Burdette	21	Spahn	143	Buhl	2.86
									Spahn	21				

THE 1959 DODGERS-WHITE SOX SERIES

Opposite top: *Dodgers celebrate their 1959 world championship. From left: Don Drysdale, who won Game Three; Chuck Essegian, who set a Series record with two pinch-hit homers; and Johnny Klippstein, who pitched two shutout innings in relief.*

Opposite bottom: *Game action in the idiosyncratic Los Angeles Memorial Coliseum. Even enormous crowds seemed sparse in the cavernous Coliseum, which was an awkwardly adapted football stadium.*

Above: *Chicago's Early Wynn throws the first pitch of the Series to the Dodgers' Junior Gilliam. The White Sox won the opener 11-0.*

Right: *Chicago's Luis Aparicio steals second in Game Four, while Maury Wills takes John Roseboro's late throw. It was one of only two steals the "Go-Go" White Sox managed all Series against Roseboro. "Roseboro took the go-go-go out of the White Sox and changed it to stop-stop-stop," wrote Yankee manager Casey Stengel, who was covering the Series for* Life. *"Now this is an outstanding thing because it hurt their style of play and what's more disrupted their spirit."*

A KEYSTONE DECADE
Great Second Basemen of the Fifties

Opposite: *A brilliant all-around player and leader, Hall of Famer Red Schoendienst helped the Cards win a pennant in 1946 and the Braves win ones in 1957-58.*

Right: *The heart of the "Go-Go" White Sox, choke-up-hitting Nellie Fox forged unforgettable DP combinations with Chico Carrasquel and Luis Aparicio. Among his many records were most years leading the league in putouts (10), total chances (9), and singles (8). He was also the third most difficult batter to strike out in baseball history.*

Below: *Pittsburgh's Bill Mazeroski, here forcing the Cardinals' Dal Maxvill, was called "No Touch" because he got rid of the ball so quickly he hardly seemed to touch it. "Bill Mazeroski's defensive statistics are probably the most impressive of any player at any position," Bill James wrote in his* Historical Baseball Abstract.

PERFECTION
Epic Feats and Characters of the Decade

Opposite top: *Yankee Don Larsen throws a called strike three past Dodger pinch hitter Dale Mitchell to complete his perfect game in the 1956 World Series.*

Opposite bottom: *Willie Mays, here beating a pickoff throw back to third, was arguably the most exciting player of the decade with his basket catch and flashy running style, complete with his hat often flying off his head. The first member of the 30-30 Club – 30 homers and 30 steals in a season – he probably ran down 30 fly balls a year no one else could have. "The only man who could have caught the ball," one announcer said of him, "just hit it."*

Above left: *Manager Casey Stengel popularized platooning, pinch hitting, and the use of late-inning relief pitchers. His Yankees won eight pennants and six world championships in the fifties.*

Above right: *The Browns' manager Zack Taylor ties a shoe for 50-pound, 3' 7" Eddie Gaedel, the midget that promoter-owner Bill Veeck used for a single trip to the plate in 1951. Naturally, he walked.*

Right: *Yankee catcher Yogi Berra bear-hugs Don Larsen, whose perfect game had just made him a baseball immortal, with a 30-40 lifetime record.*

WHY THE NATIONAL LEAGUE WAS BEST
Black NL Stars of the Fifties

Above: *The Cubs' Ernie Banks set a record for homers by shortstops with 47 in 1958. An ebullient performer for a series of non-contending Cub teams – even when he was MVP in 1958 and 1959 they finished fifth – "Mr. Cub" was best known for his pet expression, "Let's play two!"*

Left: *Future Hall of Famers Monte Irvin and Willie Mays as pennant-winning Giants in 1951, Mays's rookie year.*

Opposite top: *Catcher Roy Campanella (left) and pitcher Don Newcombe were an awesome battery for the Dodgers. Newcombe was a 20-game winner three times; Campy made the Hall.*

Opposite bottom: *Frank Robinson broke in with the 1956 Reds, led the league with 122 runs and quickly established himself as one of the greatest leaders in baseball history.*

Pages 196-7: *The first black player in the American League, Larry Doby broke in with the 1947 Indians and helped them win flags in 1948 and 1954. In 1952 he became the first black home run champion, with 32.*

First Blacks with Major League Teams

Team	Player	Date
National League		
Brooklyn Dodgers	★Jackie Robinson	4-15-1947
New York Giants	Henry Thompson	7-8-1949
	★Monte Irvin	7-8-1949
Boston Braves	Sam Jethroe	4-18-1950
Chicago Cubs	★Ernie Banks	9-17-1953
Pittsburgh Pirates	Curt Roberts	4-13-1954
St. Louis Cardinals	Tom Alston	4-13-1954
Cincinnati Reds	Nino Escalera	4-17-1954
Philadelphia Phillies	John Kennedy	4-22-1957
American League		
Cleveland Indians	Larry Doby	7-5-1947
St. Louis Browns	Henry Thompson	7-17-1947
Chicago White Sox	Minnie Minoso	5-1-1951
Philadelphia Athletics	Bob Trice	9-6-1953
New York Yankees	Elston Howard	4-14-1955
Detroit Tigers	Ossie Virgil	6-6-1958
Boston Red Sox	Pumpsie Green	7-21-1959
★Hall of Fame Member		

GIVING BASEBALL THE BUSINESS
Turning from the Game to the Business

Opposite: *Baseball has always been linked to our national culture. Here President Eisenhower throws out the first ball at the 1956 World Series. Commissioner Ford Frick, who served from 1951 through 1965, is at his left. The managers are Casey Stengel (left) and Walter Alston.*

Above right: *Three of the men who helped to make modern baseball the big business it has become. From left: National League President Warren Giles; Branch Rickey, who helped build the Cardinals, Dodgers and Pirates; and Larry MacPhail, the great Reds, Dodgers and Yankees executive.*

Right: *Walter O'Malley inspects the Los Angeles Coliseum in May 1957 – soon to be the Dodgers' new home. O'Malley's business decision to move the beloved Bums from Brooklyn earned him the hatred of many, but made major league baseball on the West Coast a reality.*

DECADE HIGHLIGHTS

Decade Leaders, 1950-59				
	National League		American League	
Batting				
BA	Stan Musial	.330	Ted Williams	.336
HRs	Duke Snider	326	Mickey Mantle	280
RBIs	Duke Snider	1031	Yogi Berra	997
Hits	Richie Ashburn	1875	Nellie Fox	1832
Runs	Duke Snider	970	Mickey Mantle	994
2B	Stan Musial	356	Minnie Minoso	259
SB	Willie Mays	179	Minnie Minoso	167
BB	Stan Musial	842	Mickey Mantle	893
Pitching				
Wins	Warren Spahn	202	Early Wynn	188
ERA	Warren Spahn	2.92	Whitey Ford	2.66
SO	Robin Roberts	1516	Early Wynn	1544
IP	Robin Roberts	3012	Early Wynn	2562

Opposite: *Despite missing parts of four seasons with injuries or for military service, an aging Ted Williams was still a major player in the fifties. In 1958 he won his last batting title, with a .388 average.*

Above: *Taking the concept of light relief to extremes, the Browns' president Bill Veeck trotted in Eddie Gaedel to hit in 1951. Though his contract was legal, American League officials banned future use of pocket-sized players.*

Right: *The three DiMaggio brothers – Joe, Vince and Dom – pose in San Francisco. In 1951, Joe's last year playing ball, Red Sox Dom (on right) belted in one more RBI, with 72, than did his famous brother.*

Page 202: *Rocky Colavito hit a record-tying four homers in one game during the 1959 season, when he led the American League with 42 dingers. Rocky had a lot going for himself: He could throw like a howitzer and had matinee-idol looks. The Indians traded him in the sixties and were never the same again.*

Page 203: *Preacher Roe went 22-3 for the 1951 Dodgers. His .880 winning percentage that year was the highest for any 20-game winner.*

On October 13, 1960, Pittsburgh looked like the Fourth of July. When Bill Mazeroski homered in the ninth inning to give the Pirates a 10-9 win over the Yankees in the seventh and final game of the World Series, people snake-danced down the streets and stalled trolleys by throwing tons of paper out windows, while worried police closed bridges and tunnels, and swamped hotel managers closed their lobbies. Mazeroski's climactic shot – the only homer ever to end a Series – concluded an era in baseball history. It was the final blow of the two-league, 16-team format that had been in existence all century. When the American League added teams in Washington and Los Angeles and moved the Senators to Minnesota in 1961, and when National League teams sprang up in New York and Houston in 1962, baseball headed down the road to the current D-days of summer: dilution, domes, divisional play and (starting in the '70s) designated hitters.

Despite Mazeroski's homer, the sixties were not known for offense. Granted, there was one last batting boom in 1961, when the Yanks' Roger Maris hit a record 61 homers and many others fed off weak expansion pitching. The best all-around hitter was Detroit's Norm Cash, who led the American League with a .361 average, homered 41 times, and drove in 132 runs. But the batting phenomenon was short-lived. In 1962 Cash's average dropped 118 points, the most ever for a reigning batting champion, and only three players had more than 40 dingers. Hitting continued to slip throughout the decade, until another round of expansion and a rules change righted the balance in 1969.

Baseball historian Bill James lists fully half a dozen explanations for the batting bust. 1) Too many homer-happy players swung for the fences. 2) On January 26, 1963, the rules committee expanded the strike zone to stretch from the bottoms of the knees to the tops of the shoulders (it had previously measured from the tops of the knees to the armpits). 3) There was more night ball than ever (hitters generally prefer batting during the day because they claim the visibility is better). 4) New stadiums – eight ballparks were built in Los Angeles, San Francisco, New York, Houston, Anaheim, Atlanta, St. Louis and San Diego – tended to move fans further from players, increasing fielders' range in foul ground. 5) Gloves got bigger and bigger. 6) And pitching mounds, poorly regulated, grew higher and higher.

Enter the prime pitching decade of golden-age baseball. Power pitchers dominated: Juan Marichal averaged 19 wins, Denny McLain went 31-6 in 1968 for the only 30-win season of the postwar period, and Bob Gibson's pitching was even better that year (22-9, 1.12 ERA). Some historians claim Sandy Koufax, who won five consecutive ERA titles in 1962-66, was in his prime the most dominating moundsman ever. Others say Gibson's '68 pitching represented the best season in baseball history. With relievers like Hall-of-Fame workhorse Hoyt Wilhelm, who averaged 56 games a season, it was no wonder the new (if unofficial) save statistic was gaining credibility.

Dominating pitchers could be a thrill to watch, especially when they did things like strike out a record 17 batters in a Series game, which Gibson accomplished in the '68 opener. In the absence of wait-for-the-homer strategy, managers had to manage and players had to manufacture runs. This is what's known as interesting baseball. Speed was back with a vengeance: In 1962 the Dodgers' Maury Wills set a then-single-season record of 104 stolen bases. Some of history's greatest fielders – the

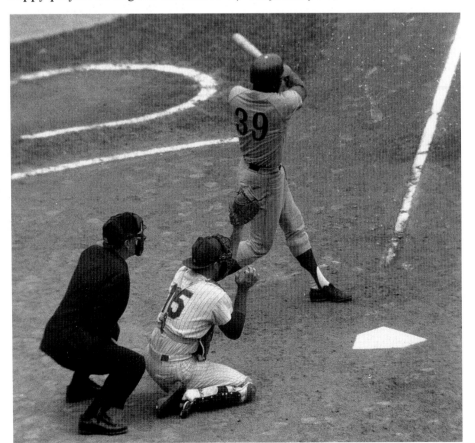

Pages 204-5: *The A's Campy Campaneris steals second against the Yankees, reaching the bag ahead of the tag by Yankee shortstop Tommy Tresh. The speed game was back in the sixties, and Campaneris led the American League in steals four years, uh, running (1965-8).*

Left: *Coco Laboy of the Expos batting against the Mets. World chumps in '62, the Mets were world champions seven years later.*

Opposite: *Twin catcher Earl Battey tags out the Tigers' Norm Cash during a game played in 1962, the Twins' second year in Minnesota. In 1965 Minnesota won its first pennant.*

Pirates' Roberto Clemente (right field) and Mazeroski (second base), the Orioles' Brooks Robinson (third base) and the Orioles' and White Sox' Luis Aparicio (shortstop) spring to mind – were in their primes.

The sixties, in fact, were a decade of miracles and wonders. Fully seven of the 10 World Series were superb shows. The Red Sox' 1967 pennant after a ninth-place finish was known as the Impossible Dream; Carl Yastrzemski, who won the last Triple Crown in baseball history that year, whipped the panting Sox horse home with probably the greatest clutch hitting ever seen. The 1969 champions were the aptly-named Miracle Mets.

The Houston Astrodome opened in 1965 with its roof and cheerleading scoreboard ("Charge!!!"); when grass wouldn't grow under the dome, the major leagues' first artificial playing surface was installed. Run-away club profits contrasted sharply with a horribly underpaid work force. In 1962 the Dodgers made a profit of $4,347,177 while paying 25-game winner Don Drysdale $35,000. Four years later the Players Association began correcting the imbalance by hiring Marvin Miller as their executive director.

It was even a decade for armchair fans. The sixties may have boasted the century's greatest baseball literature, as per witness *The Long Season* by Jim Brosnan, *Eight Men Out* by Eliot Asinov, *The Universal Baseball Association, Inc.: J. Henry Waugh, Prop.* by Robert Coover, the first edition of *The Baseball Encyclopedia*, and the greatest baseball book ever written, *The Glory of Their Times*, by Lawrence S. Ritter.

Nonetheless, the hitting drought couldn't be ignored forever. In 1968 Yastrzemski won the American League batting title with a .301 average, the lowest ever. Accordingly, the mound was lowered and the strike zone re-

duced for the 1969 season. It also helped hitters that baseball added four teams – the Montreal Expos and San Diego Padres in the NL, the Seattle Pilots and Kansas City Royals (the A's had moved to Oakland in 1968) in the AL – and began divisional play. Amid another run of weak expansion pitching, Minnesota's Rod Carew (.332) and Cincy's Pete Rose (.348) led their leagues with respectable averages.

Yet baseball purists were delighted that pitching and defense made the difference. Why did the lowly New York Mets climb to first in 1969? ". . .The only circumstance that mattered was that the expansion draft to stock the new teams had left all other contenders with at least one glaring weakness, while leaving the Mets relatively untouched," David Nemec wrote in *The Ultimate Baseball Book*. "A ninth-place club in 1968, the Mets nevertheless already had the making of the league's best pitching staff. Operating the following summer with an extra year's experience under their belts, young Mets pitchers grew stronger as the season wore on, while older pitching staffs in the league were tiring. Even so, the deciding issue was not pitching but center-field play. A rejuvenated Tommie Agee – once the American League's Rookie of the Year but a disappointment ever since – gave the Mets their first quality player at the position. . . ."

When the Mets upset the Orioles in the '69 Series, Agee made a couple of sparkling catches in center, and rightfielder Ron Swoboda turned the pivotal play with a diving backhanded stab in Game Four. Afterwards, Swoboda credited the catch to a fielding drill taught him by former Mets manager Casey Stengel. It is no surprise that Stengel influenced all five Golden Decades. The national pastime hasn't been the same without him.

BEST SEVENTH GAME?
The Great 1960 World Series Finale

Left: *A 20-game winner in 1960, Pirate Vernon Law won the first and fourth games of the 1960 Series. Shown here pitching in Game Seven, he allowed three Yankee runs in five innings before being lifted after two batters in the sixth.*

Below: *Three batters later, Yogi Berra is congratulated after hitting a three-run homer off Roy Face to put the Yankees up 5-4.*

Opposite top: *The Pirate pitchers of the moment, saver Roy Face (left) and winner Harvey Haddix, flank second baseman Bill Mazeroski after his two-run double provided the winning margin in Pittsburgh's 5-2 Game Five victory.*

Opposite bottom: *Mazeroski scores after homering to win Game Seven 10-9. It was the only circuit clout ever to end a World Series, and it concluded the most stirring seventh game ever.*

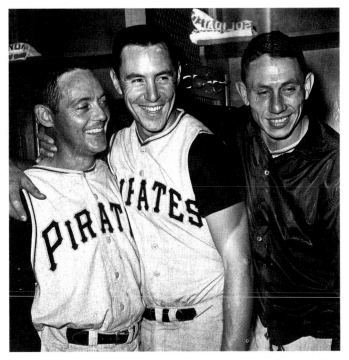

Thrilling World Series 7th Games

Year	Winner-Loser	How decided
1924	Wash-NYG	12th Inn. bad-hop single
1926	St.L-NYY	7th Inn. strikeout by Alexander
1934	St.L-Det	11-0 blowout with riot in 6th Inn.
1940	Cin-Det	2 runs in 7th Inn. overcame 1-0 lead
1945	Det-Chi	5 runs in 1st Inn. decided the game
1946	St.L-Bos	Slaughter scored from first on a double
1947	NYY-Brk	Relievers went 7⅔ innings as Yanks overcame 2-0 lead
1955	Brk-NYY	2-0 Podres shutout, 1st Dodger win
1957	Mil-NYY	7-hit Burdette shutout for his third Series victory
1958	NYY-Mil	4 runs in 8th Inn. broke a 2-2 tie
1960	Pit-NYY	9th Inn. HR by Mazeroski
1964	St.L-NYY	Gibson won with a CG despite yielding 9 hits and 5 runs
1965	LA-Minn	3-hit Koufax shutout on 2-days rest
1967	St.L-Bos	Gibson won his 3rd Series game 7-2
1968	Det-St.L	7th Inn. misjudged triple broke up a scoreless tie; Lolich won his 3rd

TRULY AN ALL-AMERICAN GAME
Baseball Expands West, Southwest, Midwest and Even East

Opposite top: *The first team photo of the 1962 New York Mets, who set a record for futility (40-120).*

Opposite bottom: *In 1960 NL President Warren Giles pointed to plans for a proposed new stadium in Houston. With him are (from left) George Kirksey, executive secretary of the Houston Sports Association; Judge Roy Hofheinz, the former mayor of Houston; and Craig Cullinen, Jr., chairman of the Houston Sports Association. In 1962 the city landed an expansion franchise, and in 1965 the Astrodome opened, looking much the way it was pictured.*

Above: *The Twins' Earl Battey reaches third with a triple in 1961, the club's first year in Minnesota. Owner Cal Griffith took advantage of plans for major league expansion and moved his Washington Senators to Minneapolis.*

Page 212-13: *Shea Stadium, home of the New York Mets.*

Franchise	League	Year	High	Finish	Year	Low	Finish
Milwaukee	NL	1960	1,497,799	2nd	1965	555,584	5th
Atlanta		1966	1,539,801	5th	1968	1,126,540	5th
Los Angeles	NL	1962	2,755,184	2nd	1968	1,581,093	7th
Chicago	NL	1969	1,674,993	2nd	1962	609,802	9th
Cincinnati	NL	1961	1,117,603	1st	1968	733,354	4th
Houston	NL	1965★	2,151,470	9th	1964	725,773	9th
Montreal	NL	1969	1,212,608	6th	–		
New York	NL	1969	2,175,373	1st	1962	922,530	10th
Philadelphia	NL	1964	1,425,891	2nd	1969	519,414	5th
Pittsburgh	NL	1960	1,705,828	1st	1968	693,485	6th
St. Louis	NL	1967	2,090,145	1st	1961	855,305	5th
San Diego	NL	1969	512,970	6th	–		
San Francisco	NL	1960	1,795,356	5th	1968	837,220	2nd
Baltimore	AL	1966	1,203,366	1st	1963	774,343	4th
Boston	AL	1968	1,940,788	4th	1965	652,201	9th
California	AL	1966★★	1,400,321	6th	1965	566,727	7th
Chicago	AL	1960	1,644,460	3rd	1969	589,546	5th
Cleveland	AL	1960	950,985	4th	1963	562,507	5th
Detroit	AL	1968	2,031,847	1st	1964	816,139	4th
Kansas City	AL	1960	774,944	8th	1965	528,344	10th
Oakland		1968	837,466	6th	1969	778,232	2nd
2 Kansas City	AL	1969	902,414	4th	–		
New York	AL	1961	1,747,725	1st	1969	1,067,996	5th
Seattle	AL	1969	677,944	6th	–		
Washington	AL	1960	743,404	5th	–		
Minnesota		1967	1,483,547	2nd	1968	1,143,257	7th
2 Washington	AL	1969	918,106	4th	1963	535,604	10th

★*Astrodome opened*
★★*Moved to new park in Anaheim, California*

TRULY AN INTERNATIONAL GAME
More Expansion, Including to Canada

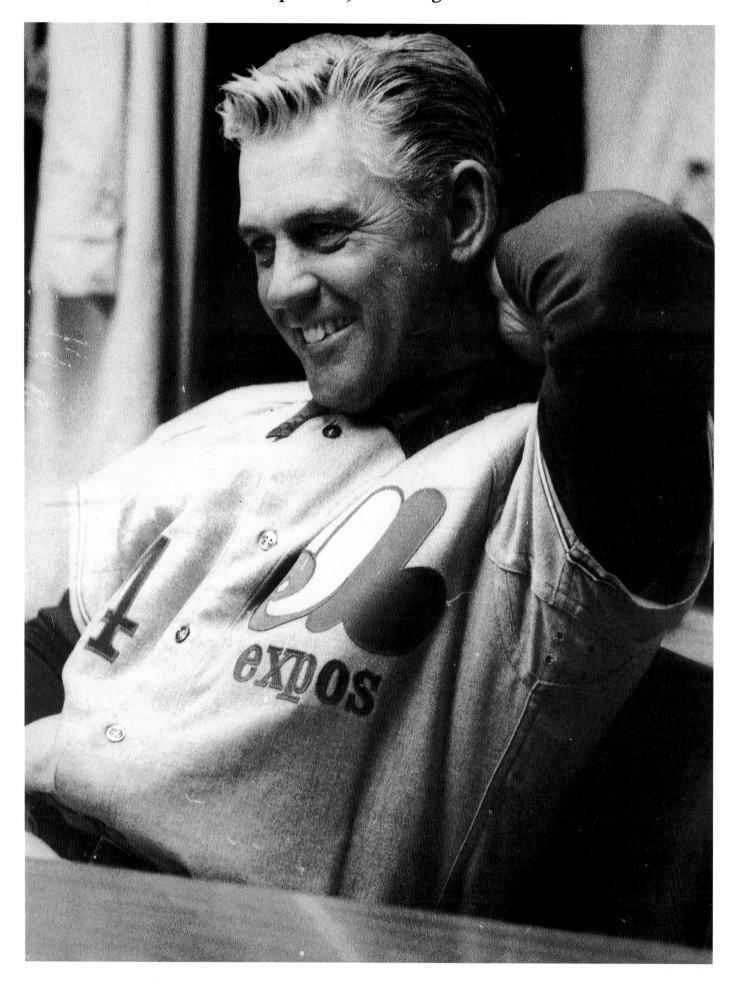

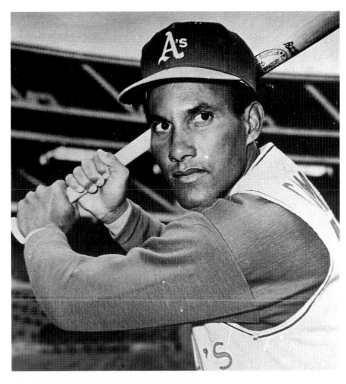

Opposite: *The major leagues expanded into Canada in 1969, with a National League team in Montreal. Here is new Expo manager Gene Mauch.*

Above: *The Mets' shortstop Bud Harrelson completes a double play against San Diego in 1969, the Padres' rookie season. The two new NL clubs, Expos and Padres, occupied the cellars of their respective divisions, 48 and 41 games behind. Better days were ahead.*

Above right: *The Athletics' shortstop Bert "Campy" Campaneris made the westward trek in '68, when the A's moved from Kansas City to Oakland.*

Right: *The American League's new Kansas City Royals franchise in 1969 featured Rookie of the Year Lou Piniella in left field.*

THE BABE UNDER ATTACK
Long-time Records Broken in '61

Above: *Mickey Mantle, here homering in the 1960 World Series, hit 54 more when bats boomed all over baseball in 1961.*

Left: *Quieting those big bats, the Yankees' Whitey Ford threw 14 shutout innings in the '61 Series, when the Yankees won in five games and the Reds hit .206. Ford extended his Series scoreless innings streak to 32, breaking one of Babe Ruth's cherished records.*

Opposite top: *Ford (left), Mantle and Roger Maris were the Big Three in the '61 Yankee pennant drive. Ford went 25-4, Mantle added 112 RBIs and a league-leading 126 walks and .687 slugging average to his 54 taters, and MVP Maris set the all-time standard with 61 homers while driving in a league-pacing 142 runs.*

Opposite bottom: *Mantle (left) and Maris were friendly rivals for the home run mark.*

THAT CLOSE
Giants Almost Win '62 Series

Opposite top: *Giant pitcher Jack Sanford throws the first pitch of Game Two in the '62 Series to Yankee leadoff batter Tony Kubek. Sanford shut the Yanks down, 2-0, allowing only three hits.*

Opposite bottom: *The Giants' Willie McCovey homering in the seventh inning of the '62 Series' second game. McCovey ended the Series on a losing note with a liner caught by Yankee second baseman Bobby Richardson. Afterwards McCovey visited a downtown jazz bar to unwind. Duke Ellington's band noticed him in the audience and played a Duke classic. Only they renamed it, "You Hit It Good, And That Ain't Bad."*

Right: *"Stretch" McCovey shows the form that earned his nickname, as Yankee Bobby Richardson is safe at first in Game Five. The Yanks won, 5-3, to take a one-game lead.*

Below: *Giant Chuck Hiller is mobbed after hitting a grand slam to cap the 7-3 win in Game Four.*

ARMS AND THE MEN
Great Pitchers of the Sixties

Left: *Ron Perranoski was baseball's nonpareil lefty in 1963, when he pitched in 69 games, won 16, saved 21, and had a stingy 1.67 ERA.*

Below: *Bob Gibson and his free-fall delivery gave baseball some unforgettable moments in 1968. Not content just to go 22-9, with a 1.12 ERA, he struck out a Series mark 17 batters – Norm Cash goes down for number 16 here – in the Cards' 4-0 win over Detroit.*

Opposite: *Tiger pitcher Denny McLain is embraced by teammate Willie Horton after winning his 30th game of the '68 season.*

Page 222: *LA's phenomenal Sandy Koufax, here fanning Cal Neeman of the Cubs, won five straight ERA titles in 1962-66. His fourth no-hitter, vs. the Cubs on September 9, 1965, was a perfect game.*

Page 223: *San Francisco's Juan Marichal was the decade leader with 191 wins. He is shown here shutting out the Mets in May 1967 for his 18th consecutive win.*

300-game Winners Beginning their Careers in the 1960s			
Player	Won-Lost	ERA	Begin-End
Don Sutton	324-256	3.26	1966-1988
Steve Carlton	329-244	3.22	1965-1988
Tom Seaver	311-205	2.86	1967-1986
Nolan Ryan	314-278	3.16	1966-1991**
Phil Niekro	318-274	3.35	1964-1987
Gaylord Perry	314-265	3.10	1962-1983

**still active

THE IMPOSSIBLE DREAM
Red Sox Win '67 Pennant

Above: *Boston's Jose Tartabull grounds out to lead off Game Three of the '67 Series. Cardinal pitcher Nelson Briles held the Sox to seven hits for a 5-2 win.*

Left: *Jim Lonborg anchored the pitching end of the Impossible Dream with a 22-9 dream season of his own, then won two games in the World Series. The magic finally ran out when he had to pitch Game Seven on only two days' rest. The Cardinals and Bob Gibson beat him 7-2.*

Opposite top: *Boston's Carl Yastrzemski won baseball's last Triple Crown in 1967, with a .326 average, 44 homers and 121 RBIs. He went 23 for 44 in the final two weeks of the season, helping the Sox win a tight three-way pennant race. Then Yaz batted .400, homered three times and slugged .840 in the Series.*

Opposite: *Yaz could also play a mean left field, as he demonstrated by robbing Curt Flood in the Series opener.*

OUT WITH THE OLD. . .
Great Oldsters Ending their Careers

Left: *After vowing he'd never remove his hat to the fans, Ted Williams gave in on September 26, 1960, his last day as an active player. The Splendid Splinter bowed out in typical style, though: He homered in his last at bat and refused to come out for a curtain call. "Gods," wrote John Updike, "do not write letters."*

Below: *Casey Stengel ended his amazin' career by managing the 1962-65 Mets. He was a much better show than his consistently poor teams. Once, when he was taking a cab with some writers, the driver asked, "Are you fellows players?" Stengel replied: "No. Neither are my players players."*

Opposite top: *The Mets' Richie Ashburn and Philadelphia's second baseman Tony Taylor await umpire Vince Smith's verdict. With a hop, skip and a jump, Smith called Ashburn out. But the 35-year-old Met ended his National League career in '62 with plenty of bounce (.306) in his bat. He even hit a career-high seven homers.*

Opposite bottom: *Duke Snider kneels next to fellow Hall of Famer Roy Campanella during a 1963 reunion of old Dodgers. Standing from left: Tommy Holmes, Carl Furillo, Gil Hodges, Don Newcombe, Cal Abrams and Ralph Branca.*

Regulars Who Hit .300 in their Last Year (1919-1969)

Year	Player-Team	Avg.	Age	LifeAvg
1920	Ray Chapman-Cle	.303	29	.278
1920	Hap Felsch-Chi	.338	29	.293
1920	Joe Jackson-Chi	.382	31	.356
1920	Buck Weaver-Chi	.333	30	.272
1924	Del Pratt-Det	.303	36	.292
1926	Ross Youngs-NYG	.306	29	.322
1927	Jack Tobin-Bos	.310	35	.309
1928	Ty Cobb-Phi	.323	41	.367
1930	George Sisler-Bos	.309	37	.340
1930	Curt Walker-Cin	.307	34	.304
1933	John Hodapp-Bos	.312	28	.311
1945	Al Cuccinello-Chi	.308	37	.280
1960	Ted Williams-Bos	.316	42	.344
1962	Richie Ashburn-NYM	.306	35	.308

. . .AND IN WITH THE NEW
New Faces of the Late Sixties

Opposite: *Baltimore manager Earl Weaver is given the heave-ho by umpire Ed Runge after protesting a balk call. The peppery Weaver took over the Orioles in 1968 and won six divisional titles, four pennants and one world championship in the next 12 years. Though he was known for relying on "pitching and the three-run homer," he was an innovator who pioneered use of computer charts.*

Right: *Twenty-three and clean-shaven, Reggie Jackson took a shot at home-run immortality for the 1969 A's. He led the league in slugging percentage, with 47 homers and 118 RBIs.*

Below: *Tagged out trying to stretch a double, Reggie had 36 two-baggers and 13 stolen bases in '69.*

Page 230: *At 22, then-Met Nolan Ryan got a save in the '69 Series.*

Page 231: *The promising Reds' catcher Johnny Bench was Rookie of the Year in 1968.*

PLAYERS COME OF AGE
The Players' Union Gets Strong

Salary Increases			
Year	Rookie (min)	Average	Avg. Worker
1967	$ 6,000	$ 19,000	$ 5,878
1969	10,000	24,909	6,456
1971	12,750	31,543	7,298
1973	15,000	36,566	8,103
1975	16,000	44,676	9,556
1980	30,000	143,756	13,391
1983	35,700	289,194	17,238
1985	60,000	371,571	18,697
1988	62,500	438,729	21,112

Opposite top: *Marvin Miller (left), new executive director of the Major League Baseball Players' Association, speaks with player reps Clete Boyer of the Yankees and Roy McMillan of the Mets in 1966. With an experienced union man at their helm, the players soon gained concessions.*

Opposite bottom: *Dodger general manager Buzzy Bavasi (second from left) announces an agreement with pitchers Don Drysdale (left) and Sandy Koufax (to Bavasi's left) in March 1966. The meeting ended their joint holdout when they signed for a package estimated at $230,000.*

Right: *Cardinal outfielder Curt Flood reaches for a long fly. In 1969 he reached even higher, going to court to challenge the reserve clause. Although Flood lost his case in the Supreme Court, his suit opened the door to change.*

BIG AND BAD TRADES

Opposite top: *Frank Robinson beats it back to third on a pick-off attempt. Some thought Robinson was an "old 30" when the Reds traded him to Baltimore after the 1965 season. The hustling rightfielder promptly won a Triple Crown and MVP Award.*

Opposite bottom: *Lou Brock steals second against the Pirates. In a lopsided trade, the Cubs dealt speedster Lou Brock and others to the Cardinals for pitcher Ernie Broglio and others, in 1964. Broglio won seven games in three years; Brock played 16 more seasons, retired with 3,023 hits, and led the NL in stolen bases eight times. Talk about a steal.*

Right: *In '66 the Phillies traded Ferguson Jenkins to the Cubs. He went on to have seven 20-win seasons.*

Below: *Joey Jay, late of the Braves, joined the Reds with Juan Pizarro in 1961 (in exchange for Roy McMillan) and spun off two straight 21-win seasons.*

Below right: *A Giant embarrassment: trading Orlando Cepeda to the Cards, for Ray Sadecki, in 1966. Next year he was MVP.*

CRASS OR COMFY?
Baseball Turns Commercial

Opposite: *The suburban-style neatness of such newer ballparks as Dodger Stadium contrasts with quaint and colorful urban gems, as was Ebbets Field. The face of baseball changed rapidly in the sixties, and it seemed that some of the game's gritty charm was fading.*

Right: *Fenway's "Green Monster" – the left-field wall – is a remaining bit of baseball antiquity. Its familiar hand-operated scoreboard is now supplemented by an electronic one above the bleachers.*

Below: *The Houston Astrodome opened in 1965. The following year the Astrodome became the first ballpark to be laid with Astroturf. The stadium's "exploding" scoreboard also became a fixture in other parks.*

Below right: *Bowie Kuhn became commissioner in 1969 and turned baseball from a pastime into a product with his support of such schemes as a relief award named after an antacid.*

TIGERS IN THE GRASS
The Great 1968 Tiger Team

Opposite top: *First baseman Norm Cash hit .385 to lead the Tigers in the 1968 Series.*

Opposite bottom: *Detroit's veteran rightfielder Al Kaline hits a two-run homer in Game Three of the 1968 Series. Kaline had two roundtrippers and eight RBIs in seven games.*

Above: *Series MVP Mickey Lolich, 3-0 with a 1.67 ERA, outdueled the Cardinals' Bob Gibson in a thrilling Game Seven.*

Above right: *Tiger shortstop Mickey Stanley tags out the Cardinals' Curt Flood after Lolich picked Flood off first base in Game Seven. Shifted from center field shortly before the Series, Stanley made the difficult transition to save the Tigers' skins.*

Right: *Denny McLain's 31 wins in '68 earned him runaway selection as American League MVP.*

UNSUNG BUT SPECTACULAR
Unheralded Players Who Made Major Contributions

Left: *Supposedly washed-up, Moe Drabowsky allowed only one hit in six and two-thirds innings and struck out a Series relief record 11 batters while the Orioles bested the Dodgers 5-2 in the opening game of the 1966 World Series.*

Opposite top: *The Cardinals' Tim McCarver beat the Yankees 5-2 on a three-run 10th-inning homer in the fifth game of the 1964 World Series. McCarver led all comers with a .478 average and .739 slugging percentage, scored a run and drove in another in the seventh-game clincher.*

Opposite bottom: *After homering 21 times as a part-time player during the 1961 season, John Blanchard added two more timely blasts in the Yankees' World Series win over Cincinnati. Here he is greeted at home after his two-run homer in the finale.*

A RUNNING GAME FOR REAL
Great Baserunners of the Sixties

Selected Power and Speed Leaders

Year	Player-Team	HR	SB
1961	Roger Maris-NY	61	0
1961	Mickey Mantle-NY	54	12
1962	Willie Mays-SF	49	18
1962	Harmon Killebrew-Min	48	1
1964	Harmon Killebrew-Min	49	0
1965	Willie Mays-SF	52	9
1966	Frank Robinson-Bal	49	8
1969	Harmon Killebrew-Min	49	8
1969	Frank Howard-Wash.	48	1

Year	Player-Team	SB	HR
1962	Maury Wills-LA	104	6
1965	Maury Wills-LA	94	0
1965	Lou Brock-St.L	63	16
1966	Lou Brock-St.L	74	15
1968	Lou Brock-St.L	62	6
1968	Bert Campaneris-Oak	62	4
1969	Tommy Harper-Sea	73	9
1969	Bert Campaneris-Oak	62	2

Opposite top: *More than just the finest fielding rightfielder of all time, the Pirates' Roberto Clemente was a racy baserunner. Here he scores on Willie Stargell's single when the throw home evades Cub catcher Ed Bailey.*

Opposite bottom: *Maury Wills of the Dodgers reinvented the stolen base. No one had stolen 50 since Max Carey in 1923 when Wills did it in 1960. Two years later he broke Ty Cobb's 47-year-old record with 104 (shown here taking number 47) and was elected MVP.*

Right: *Minnesota's Rod Carew steals home safely on July 16, 1969, for his seventh of the season in as many tries. The feat tied him with Pete Reiser (1946) for the all-time record.*

Below: *The Cards' Lou Brock led the National League in steals eight out of nine years (1966-74).*

Pages 244-5: *Earlier, Luis Aparicio led all American Leaguers in steals nine straight years (1956-64).*

THE MIRACLE METS
Mets Go All the Way in '69

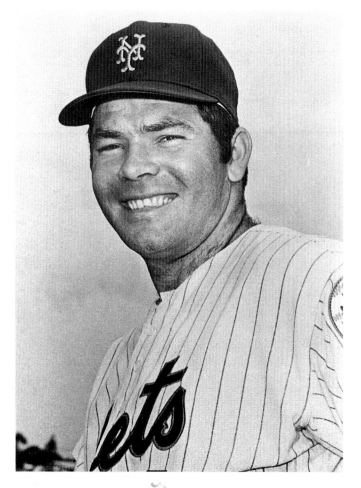

Opposite top: *In the final game of the 1969 World Series, Met manager Gil Hodges shows a smudge of shoe polish on the ball to umpire Lou DiMuro. Why the fuss? Hodges was arguing that his batter, Cleon Jones, had been hit on the foot by a pitch. Convinced, DiMuro waved him on to first, and the next batter, Donn Clendenon, homered to cut the Orioles' lead to 3-2. The Mets won 5-3.*

Opposite bottom left: *Met rightfielder Ron Swoboda made a diving catch that turned around Game Four. The Mets won it 2-1 in 10 innings to take a commanding 3-1 lead in the Series.*

Opposite bottom right: *Jerry Koosman won twice, including the Series clincher.*

Left: *Tom Seaver helped the Mets win the pennant with a league-leading 25 victories. Seaver won the Cy Young Award for his performance.*

Below: *Clendenon homering with Jones aboard in the Series finale.*

Above: *The Orioles' Mike Cuellar throws the first pitch of the '69 World Series to Tommie Agee. The Orioles won 4-1 for their lone moment of glory.*

Left: *Baltimore's Mark Belanger gets back to first after singling in Game Five. Pitcher Dave McNally followed with a homer.*

Opposite: *The Mets fight their way off the field after clinching their first world championship. They had come a long way, from nine and a half games out in mid-August, to winning the division by eight games, to sweeping Atlanta in the first divisional playoff series, to this.*

DECADE HIGHLIGHTS

Decade Leaders, 1960-69

	National League		American League	
Batting				
BA	Roberto Clemente	.328	Al Kaline	.295
HRs	Hank Aaron	375	Harmon Killebrew	393
RBIs	Hank Aaron	1107	Harmon Killebrew	1013
Hits	Roberto Clemente	1877	Brooks Robinson	1692
Runs	Hank Aaron	1091	Harmon Killebrew	864
2B	Vada Pinson	310	Carl Yastrzemski	318
AB	Maury Wills	6091	Brooks Robinson	6093
SB	Maury Wills	545	Luis Aparicio	342
BB	Ed Mathews	718	Harmon Killebrew	970
Pitching				
Wins	Juan Marichal	191	Jim Kaat	142
ERA	Sandy Koufax	2.36	Whitey Ford	2.83
SO	Bob Gibson	2071	Jim Kaat	1435
IP	Don Drysdale	2630	Jim Kaat	2224

Opposite: *The immortal Satchel Paige, at age 59, throws to a Boston batter on September 26, 1965. The Hall of Famer had a post-retirement three-inning fling for the A's so that he'd qualify for a big-league pension. He surrendered no runs and only one hit, while becoming the oldest player in major league history.*

Right: *In 1963 the Cards' Stan Musial got a rousing greeting from young fans as he began his last season.*

Below: *Carl Yastrzemski's fielding became almost as spectacular as his hitting once he mastered the mysteries of the Green Monster. Here he makes a great catch in the '67 Series opener.*

Pages 252-3: *Yogi Berra shows the form that landed him in the World Series record books. In Berra's all-time record Series games (75) and at-bats (259), he rated first in hits (71) and doubles (tied at 10), second in total bases (117), RBIs (39) and runs (41); and third in homers (12) and walks (33). The long-time Yankee catcher retired in 1965.*

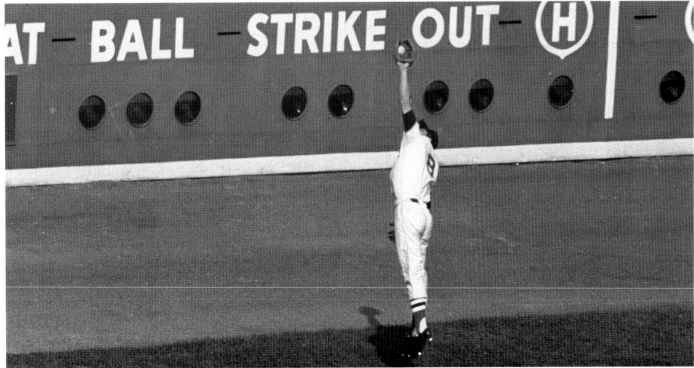

APPENDIX OF STATISTICS

INDEX

Numerals in *italics* indicate photos

ACKNOWLEDGMENTS

The author and publisher would like to thank the following people who have helped in the preparation of this book: Barbara Thrasher, who edited it; Don Longabucco, who designed it; Lloyd Johnson, who compiled the statistics; Rita Longabucco, who did the picture research; and Florence Norton, who prepared the index.

PHOTO CREDITS

All photographs courtesy of UPI/Bettmann Newsphotos, except the following:
Chicago Cubs: 131(top left).
Malcolm Emmons: 235(top).
Greer Studios, Inc: 185(top left).
Dwayne Labaacus: 235(bottom left).
National Baseball Library, Cooperstown, NY: 6, 10, 16(bottom), 17(all three), 20, 23(bottom left), 24(top, bottom left), 26-27, 29(center left), 33(top), 35(top, center), 36(both), 37(top), 38(bottom), 39(bottom both), 40, 41(all three), 44(both), 45(top left, top right), 47(both), 50(all three), 51(both), 52-53, 54, 55(bottom), 61, 62(all three), 66(bottom both), 68(bottom left), 69, 71, 74, 75(bottom both), 76(top right), 80(top right), 81(both), 82(top), 85, 87(top), 92(bottom), 93(both), 96(bottom both), 98(top), 100, 101(top left, bottom), 105, 118, 119(bottom), 124(bottom), 125(top), 131(top right, bottom), 143(all three), 149(top), 153(bottom), 160, 171(top), 177, 179(top right), 187(top), 190, 191(top), 195(bottom), 202, 203, 209(bottom), 215(top right), 220(top), 224(bottom), 230, 231, 233, 234(bottom), 235(bottom right), 239(top left), 243(bottom), 246(bottom both), 247(top).
Photofile, Inc: 11(bottom).
TOPPS Chewing Gum: 2(all nine), 11(top both), 217(top three).
US Marine Corps: 123.